Dear Charlie

Letters to My Children

Christopher Kimball

Multnomah Publishers *Sisters, Oregon*

DEAR CHARLIE
published by Multnomah Publishers, Inc.

© 1999 by Christopher Kimball
International Standard Book Number: 1–57673–490–0

Cover photograph courtesy of Christopher Kimball
Design by David Uttley Design

Scripture quotations are taken from:
The Holy Bible, New International Version (NIV) © 1973, 1984 by International Bible
Society. Used by permission of Zondervan Publishing House.
Multnomah is a trademark of Multnomah Publishers, Inc., and is registered in the U.S.
Patent and Trademark Office.
The colophon is a trademark of Multnomah Publishers, Inc.

Printed in the United States

For information:
Multnomah Publishers, Inc., Post Office Box 1720, Sisters, Oregon 97759
Library of Congress Cataloging-in-Publication Data
Kimball, Christopher.
Dear Charlie: letters to my children / by Chris Kimball.
p. cm.
ISBN 1-57673-490-0 (alk. paper)
1. Kimball, Christopher Correspondence. 2. Parents—Vermont Correspondence.
3. Parent and child—Vermont Miscellanea. 4. Family—Vermont Miscellanea.
5. Country life—Vermont Miscellanea. 6. Conduct of life. I. Title.
HQ755.8.K558 1999
306.874'09743—dc21
99-35206 CIP
99 00 01 02 03 04 05 06 — 10 9 8 7 6 5 4 3 2 1

FOR

Whitney, Caroline, Charlie,
and Emily

Contents.

3. Simple Pleasures

4. Lessons Learned

5. Life on the Farm

6. Times of Celebration and Remembrance

7. Amazing Grace

*"The great man is he who does not
lose his child's heart."*

MENCIUS, 371–289 B.C.

Acknowledgments.

Many adventures in life begin with a phone call from a stranger, and this book is no exception. Two years ago, Matt Jacobson, then with Multnomah Publishers, called to say he had read a letter to my son, Charlie, which was published as an editorial in my publication, *Cook's Illustrated.* He went on to suggest that I write a collection of letters to my children. I want to thank Matt for his support and enthusiasm.

I also want to thank everyone at Multnomah who has helped with this project, especially Don Jacobson, Keith Wall, and Steve Curley. It is rare to find a group of people who have married their beliefs to their profession, recognizing that money is not the only coin of the realm.

My wife, Adrienne, is an excellent editor in her own right and has added much to the manuscript over the years, including a keen eye for the relationship between parent and child.

I also owe a debt of gratitude to Bill Gillespie, former dean of the faculty at Phillips Exeter Academy, who spoke the following words at the 1967 commencement address: "But I hope, and I expect, that when you find yourselves involved in skirmishes on the frontiers of barbarism, which are not very far away, you'll strike some shrewd blows in favor of civilization." I have paraphrased his comments in one of my letters to Charlie.

Last, but not least, I want to thank Whitney, Caroline, Charlie, and Emily for teaching me more than I can ever teach them.

Introduction.

Each of us writes letters to our children in our mind as we watch them take little steps into their future—and ours. Yet most parents never take the time to put their thoughts down on paper. At the time, we believe that these rare moments of inspiration, when we are able to make out the outline of some grander plan, will stand the test of time. But, as all parents eventually discover, time dims even the brightest revelations, leaving a dull ache of knowledge forgotten.

My wife, Adrienne, and I have four children: Whitney, 11; Caroline, 9; Charlie, 4; and Emily, 1. When Whitney and Caroline were just a few years old, a stranger came up to me in a parking lot as I was walking my daughters to the car and said with great concern, "Before you know it, they'll be gone. Use your time well." The next thing I knew, he had vanished. This apparition and his sudden disappearance left its mark, and I began writing letters to each of my children to record particularly vivid moments when the seen and unseen worked together to shed light on the ritual of daily life. I wrote about fishing and hunting trips, Old Home Day, parades, church, and life on the farm, as well as more personal notes recording private moments with each child. A few of these letters were inspired by sermons I have delivered as a lay preacher at our small Methodist church. (When I preach, it saves the congregation the fifty-dollar fee for a guest minister.)

Most of the letters were written in Vermont, where our family has a farm. There we keep bees and grow corn, apples, potatoes, and hay. This is purely avocation as I make my living publishing and editing *Cook's Illustrated* magazine as well as authoring cookbooks. During my growing-up years, I spent summers in this small town in the Green Mountains, where I worked for a dairy farmer and helped our family raise Angus and pigs. I have found that farm life has countless benefits for children and their parents—time is forgiving, labor is shared, and each of us can put down roots that last a lifetime. As I often tell my children when they seem out of sorts, "Dig a hole and think about the possibilities!" All things are possible on the farm, where death and renewal work hand in hand, completing a cycle that is too often concealed in the bustle of modern life.

After having written a dozen or so letters, I read them one evening only to find that the tables had been turned. What had started out as advice to my children had quickly turned into a record of how they had changed my life. I discovered the great wisdom and thoughtfulness of children from Whitney, the healing warmth of unconditional love from Caroline, enthusiasm for all things from Charlie, and the blessing and sanctity of life from young Emily. That is not to say that raising children is always an exercise in mutual love and respect. Darker moments are also recorded in these pages. With the gift of hindsight, however, I have found these episodes to be equally inspiring because they require thoughtful responses and reflection as well as reassessment of what I had believed to be universal truths.

These letters were penned over a period of five years, starting when my wife and I had only two young daughters. Some letters are written expressly to one child, others to a combination or all of them. This book begins with letters written directly to each child and then one letter to all of my children about their mother. Subsequent chapters are divided into themes: small-town living, simple pleasures, lessons learned, and so on. My wife has duly noted that Whitney has garnered the largest share of letters, which, I suppose, is the benefit or burden of being the first child. However, should this volume find favor among the public, subsequent collections of letters will correct this imbalance.

The title of this book, *Dear Charlie*, was chosen because "Dear Charlie, Age 3" (the second letter in this collection) is my favorite and the one that has received the most comment over the years. It was originally published as an editorial in *Cook's Illustrated*, and the response from readers encouraged me to continue writing.

I hope that you recognize many faces in these letters: the troubled adult suddenly appearing in a child's simple face, the firm and accepting gaze of the newborn, the wild enthusiasm for living in the chatter of a four-year-old, and the stubborn determination in a glance from a younger sister. Our family is no different than any other. Viewed from afar, the routine of growing up is entirely predictable and cuts across all households. But viewed day to day from the middle of the fray, we are constantly in awe of the permutations of personality and the complexity of the moment.

I also hope that you find the familiar in these pages, moments of delight and recognition, but I also hope that you will also come across an unfamiliar thought or notion as well, a simple turn of phrase that pulls you up short for just a moment, as you reflect on what was or might have been.

PART ONE

Letters to My Children

one

Dear Charlie, age 2

"IT IS A SECOND LIFE FOR ME,
ONE THAT IS TRULY RICHER THAN THE FIRST..."

———————

When you were just two years old, you were a tangle of arms and legs pumping furiously, acting as if they had a life of their own. As your corduroys once again fell to your knees, you would announce in a cry of desperation that "my pants aren't working," trying to get a grip on the waistband, tugging and grunting to no avail. It is your rugged determination that I so love about you, a total lack of precision married to the heedless enthusiasm of a billy goat, head down, charging right into whatever life has to offer.

You are my third child, my only son, and you have been given a great spark of life, the gift of living totally in the present, unaware of the shadows that worry and weaken us, drawing us away from the spotlight. You have always run to the great outdoors, happiest under the full sun of midday, pressing on with great adventures pursued with the charm of reckless abandon. You sleep in your older sisters' room, between their beds, slipped into a wicker laundry basket, head and feet curved upward like a big trout in a small skillet. You spent all last summer dressed in only a cowboy hat, rubber boots, and diapers, chasing frogs while carelessly negotiating the uneven ground on your short, baby legs.

You are utterly without artifice or subtlety, quite happy, I expect, to declare your intentions without embellishment or go-betweens. Your raw, unfiltered being has been one of my life's great blessings. Love, pain, anger, frustration, and happiness can be read on your wide-open face in large type, big block letters spelled out for everyone to see at a distance. When you laugh hard, it is a deep, rich crescendo that starts deep in your belly and percolates its way up, exploding out of your mouth, eyes wide open, startled by the *sheer* force of it. You have been filled to the brim with the stuff of life, packed to the gills with a divine yeast that ferments and bubbles, sending you in all directions at once, popping with a great eagerness for anything life has to put in front of you.

I offer a simple thank-you for these moments—for your big bear hugs when I walk in the door, for the sword fights we have before bedtime, for the moment you came down the stairs Christmas morning and saw the bright red fire truck filled with candy that Santa brought. Your eyebrows arched skyward, eyes sprung open, and burst into a spontaneous "WOW," an eruption of joy and awe for the great mystery of it all.

You have taken me by the hand, out from the lengthening shadows of adulthood and back into the sun. It is a second life for me, one that is truly richer than the first, and it has been delivered, unexpectedly, by a two-year-old dressed only in a cowboy hat, diaper, and big green rubber boots.

two.

Dear Charlie, age 3

"THE TIME WILL COME
WHEN THE FARMHOUSE WILL BE STILL,
ABANDONED BY SMALL VOICES..."

———————

You are my first son, your two older sisters having exhibited a startling disregard for gender-neutral behavior, quickly abandoning the train set and Tonka toys (presents from Dad) in favor of bright pink Lisa Frank diaries and endless rolls of glow-in-the-dark stickers (presents from Mom). I didn't know I wanted a son until you came along one January afternoon, the plumbing merely a passing detail at the time.

But today as I sat on the half-rusted International, ploughing up the lower cornfield, you sat on my lap, lulled by the warm spring sun and the churning of the tiller, until your small body went soft, eyes half closed, rocking gently in my arms. The roar of the tractor's engine is always a call to action, sending your short legs into a frenzy of motion, racing down the driveway, calling after your dad on the big red machine. It is honest work we do together, the two of us, watching the swallows swoop over the just-ploughed fields, your dad trying frantically not to let the moments fade.

But for now, I take comfort that my life is filled with a great inventory of moments yet to be lived—our first fishing expedition, watching the sun burn through the thick, early morning mist on the Batten Kill; splitting and stacking oak and chestnut on a chilly November afternoon, the two of us working as one; our first hunt together, flushing a grouse or woodcock, the great beating of wings sending our hearts racing at the same instant. As a father of older children, I know that the innocence fades over time and the special moments are of a different sort, no less magical, but painted in more subtle, often darker hues. They come not in great waves of joy, but in single, unexpected moments; a parent's ear must be well-tuned not to miss them.

But you are still young and a boy, all bluff and swagger, without the skill or need to hide what you are really thinking. Your deepest desires are etched plainly in your smile.

Yet during these postcard summers, I am constantly reminded that the time will come when the farmhouse will be still, abandoned by small voices. I see your mother and me, standing by the stove, troubled, not knowing when we will cook for you again. The everyday noises of childhood will have faded, the tune distant, but a few melodies still remembered. But to spend precious hours stacking yet-to-be-created memories like cordwood seems to be so much time wasted. Instead, I want to burn them all now, before the memories turn soft with age, producing little heat.

Living for the moment, all the bright, crisp New England days will collapse together as one, the two of us driving the old Ford in circles in the lower meadow, laughing, banging the horn, getting stuck in mud up to the axles and not caring. We'll set aside the camera and notebook and explore old haylofts, finding great treasures—a dusty bottle of number two colic drops or an old issue of *Hoard's Dairyman*. We'll be a right pair, you and I, going everywhere, doing everything, the neighbors expecting to see your small, round face peering through the steering wheel each time I drive by. And when our summers together are over, and time enough has passed to cloud memories of frog hunts and muddy boots, bowls of homemade peach ice cream, old yellow casseroles filled with silky custard, and the crashing of thunder as we sit snug on the front porch, I will drive the old pickup down the same dirt road we traveled many summers before. On that day, you will have long said good-bye to this small town, but our neighbors will see your face in mine as I pass; happy, expectant, full of the joy of a three-year-old, eyes keen with the excitement of a new world just around the next bend.

And on another day, you will come back home to show us your trophies and scars, having struck a few shrewd blows in favor of civilization. I will search your face for a hint of your dad; the way I squint into the bright sun or your eyes reflecting a passing memory, a small wisp of smoke from that blazing fire we started so many years ago. But if I look hard and see nothing of myself, that will be no disappointment. I'll know that each time I start up the old tractor, you will be there for me, asleep in my arms, as together we plough the fields of your childhood.

three.

Dear Charlie, age 4

"WITH AGE COMES MANY THINGS,
BUT THE LEAST LOVELY OF THEM IS A
DIMINISHED APPETITE FOR ADVENTURE..."

———————

D
ad, when I get bigger, will you teach me to fly?"
you asked, quite serious about the prospect, as if
you were asking me to teach you how to ride a bike or catch
a fish.

"Well, do you know anybody who can fly?" I queried,
trying to get a bead on what was going through your mind.

"Peter Pan can fly," you shot back with total confidence.

Pursuing this conversation as far as it would go, I asked,
"Well, how do you do it?"

And out of the clear blue sky came your explanation.

"First you stretch out your arms like this. Then you think lovely thoughts. No, no!" You stopped, frustrated that you had forgotten an important step.

"First you stretch out your arms like this. Then you get Tinkerbell to sprinkle pixie dust all over you. Then you think lovely thoughts and then you fly out the window."

"And where are you flying to, Charlie?"

"Two stars to the right and straight on 'til morning."

It seems that you knew the directions to Never Never Land by heart. I should have known.

With age comes many things, but the least lovely of them is a diminished appetite for adventure, a youthful enthusiasm for heading out into the night sky with nothing more than a thin film of pixie dust and high expectations. My adult appetite for risk pales next to your heedless thrusts into the unknown. Perhaps it is nature's way of ensuring the propagation of the species. Parents ought to be risk-adverse caregivers, but you, a mere four-year-old, are still going through a process of natural selection during which an appetite for bold actions may actually enhance survival. After all, in nature the meek rarely get the lion's share of the evening meal.

I was recently confronted with a choice between long-term financial security and risk. Your refrain, "Two stars to the right and straight on 'til morning," came flooding back to me. Should middle-aged parents avoid risk in favor of protecting the family nest? It is easy to make the case for the road most traveled, the path that leads quickly and safely back home. But as your father, I must provide you with many things—not just a safe, secure childhood. Even though you do not understand it now, you need to see your parents approach life straight on, not flinching from the possibilities. Will I have you come to me in my dotage, taking me aside to wonder why I never took my chance, never stretched out my arms and looked upward for that second star to the right? I think not. I would rather risk failure than avoid risk. As your father, it is my duty to take considered risks, avoiding the foolhardy but not wincing when it is my turn at bat.

So I have taken this chance for you as well as for me, that together we can explore what life has to offer. We'll stretch out our arms, you and I, wait for a sprinkling of pixie dust, and all the while think lovely thoughts. Our future lies two stars to the right and straight on 'til morning.

four.

Dear Caroline, age 3

"LIKE GOOD FRIENDS,
THE BEST FOODS ARE THE SIMPLEST
AND MOST HONEST..."

Y ou were always a good eater. At age two, you ate your bowl of cereal, your older sister's, and then held out an empty bowl and demanded the hat trick. As with all kids, you liked what was familiar and comforting. Small bits of bright color in a sea of ivory noodles were disturbing— an invading army that had to be picked out one soldier at a time. You adored salads and fruit but mistrusted the hidden mysteries of chunky soups. You loved to cook. You kneaded bread dough with gusto until it was as satiny smooth and plump as your belly. You stood on the trash can in a diaper cutting out biscuits. You hid behind the kitchen counter and pilfered strips of pie dough. You and your sister loved to eat raw flour, licking it off the counter when my back was turned.

Now that you are reading this letter, you are older and may have your own family. These distant memories of sourdough, baked beans, corn muffins, apple pie, fresh-picked blueberries, and upside-down cake are part of your heritage. You were raised in New England and ate the foods of our neighbors. Although you will eat sashimi and soba, skate and dim sum, these are the familiar foods that make up your past.

You grew up in a time in which little was familiar. In your grandfather's day, the world was no larger than a neighborhood. The whole clan used to meet at twelve o'clock every Sunday at your great-great-great-grandmother's row house on Cathedral Street in Baltimore. Hair slicked back and shoes shined, your grandfather had to sit quietly in the thickly draped Victorian parlor with the grown-ups, bored and waiting for dinner, which was as predictable as the start of school—beaten biscuits, a roast, mashed potatoes, lima beans, and peach pie in season and a cake the rest of the year. Today, a whole generation has grown up with a take-out culture. So much of it is good and convenient, but little of it has the ring of the familiar, of being personal enough to become part of our past.

I remember midday dinner in the 1950s at the farmhouse next door in Vermont. Fresh baking powder biscuits (extras were stacked in a large tin), meat and mashed potatoes, a pitcher of fresh milk covered with a blue-and-white kitchen towel to keep out flies, a just-baked loaf of anadama bread, and molasses cookies with flour-dusted bottoms. Your grandmother worked full time even back then, and our own house had a Southern cook. Enormous pans of spoonbread, collard greens, black-eyed peas, giant popovers, and red snapper every Friday are as vivid as the day they were served.

Your mother and I think about what we should pass on to the next generation. Everyone talks values, as if they can be passed along like computer skills. We'd like to pass along memories: Thanksgiving morning, butter-dipped raw folds of Parker House Rolls; clipping sprigs of basil just before the first frost; stirring the batter for your sister's devil's food birthday cake. In food, there is so much to learn about life. Like good friends, the best foods are the simplest and most honest. Start out with memories of your dad's apple pie and then later on you can take the measure of a tart de pommes with créme anglaise. I'm betting that the deep-dish pie will stand the test of time because we made it together—your tiny hands on the axle-size rolling pin while you demanded, "Let me do it!"

Now you are reading this, you are doing it all yourself. I hope that the first splash of fall color reawakens an urge to roll out your own round of pie dough, filling it with firm, juicy Northern Spys or Macouns and dad's special spice mixture (don't forget the allspice). I hope that your best friends are as dependable and well-made as that pie. Before your mother and I got married, I invited her up for a weekend at the farm. She threw hay with the best of them and was no quitter—the last hay wagon wasn't empty until the barn swallows came out. That was the first day I knew there would be a Caroline in my future.

As for my future, I look forward to creating new memories with the next generation. You won't come to the farm as often as I'd like, but as soon as your kids can stand, they're going to get a good dose of rolling pie dough, kneading bread, and cutting cookies. Like the candyman, I'll lure them with a lick of the bowl and hook them with the magic of the kitchen. And after you've gone back home, your mom and I will sit together in front of the fire like co-conspirators with memories of small voices ringing out, "Let me do it!" Only then will we realize that, all this time, you were giving us the memories. Thank you.

five.

Dear Whitney, age 9

"IT WAS A DAY FOR HOLDING HANDS
ONE LAST TIME..."

———————————

Today, as you and I rollerbladed by the river, you skated up to my side and I felt your hand grab mine in a firm grip—not the loose, subordinate grasp of a young child, but something more assured. Whitney, you turn ten years old next month, the sweep of your thin body starting to take on the lithe, sinewy grace of a young woman. You are hovering between childhood and something greater, a world you can see but dimly. It is alternately exhilarating and frightening, the fault lines of adulthood coming into greater focus, as you sense the deeper currents that flow just below the surface of family life. Your step is less certain these days, although quicker.

The pace of life is changing, hurtling you toward a far shore that promises adventure but also confusion and disappointment.

In this moment of uncertainty, you have come up to my side and grabbed hold of my hand, perhaps for the last time. When you were young, we held hands every weekday as we walked to the school bus, your delicate fingers slipping into mine. I told you homemade stories as we walked past the row houses on Worcester Street, the stone lion on Columbus Avenue, and then through the park and on to the bus stop. On the day of the great blizzard, we bundled up against the wind and the snow falling sideways. I broke the trail through the deep drifts, and you came behind, in single file, unable to hold hands. You were anxious that day, not being able to walk side by side, but we remember it fondly. We pushed our way through the storm, peering out at the world through thick-hooded parkas, hearing only the howling of the wind and the scrunch of snow underfoot.

Now I wonder if today was the last time you will take hold of my hand without a sense of duty or tradition. The pact between father and daughter is an odd one; we need each other in different ways, a complex give and take evolving over the years. As you grow into adulthood, self-perception runs interference between the easy flow of affection bestowed from one to another. Holding hands is easily colored by other considerations, the need to grow apart arriving like a stranger at the door, one who has come calling on my little girl, to woo her away with a taste of freedom.

But if today was the final time we are to hold hands as father and daughter, I will be satisfied that it was a good day. We had our sunny afternoon, the rain finally ended, the sun bright, the breeze fresh, the couples intoxicated with the scent and feel of freshly mown grass. These few hours were an unexpected gift, arriving in the midst of a typical Saturday. The journey through side streets were just for the two of us. No stranger came between us on this bright day. It was a day for holding hands one last time, for being good company, for not having awkward silences or words unspoken. It is for these moments that I live, precious hours that tumble down from the sky when least expected. And when the day comes that I see you holding hands with another, I will give my blessing, for we have had our Saturday afternoon in early spring. We will remember with fondness that there was a time when you reached out for me, a daughter reaching out to a father, and I took your hand.

six.

To my unborn child

"STILL HIDDEN IN YOUR MOTHER'S WOMB,
YOU HAVE ARRIVED IN MY HEART..."

———————

We have yet to meet face-to-face, you and I. I don't know your name or the way your mouth curls into a smile or the sound of your newborn cry, the one that will announce your arrival into our world. But you, still hidden in your mother's womb, have arrived in my heart. You are already a member in good standing of this family, a presence, a little person who sits with us at the dinner table, who enters into our conversations, whose small feet even push at your mother's tummy, your brother and sisters watching awestruck as you somersault in your dreams. As I write this, your name may be Emily, Mary Alice, Hilary, Jennifer, or Katy. But nameless, you are no less a blessing, a life already in existence, the ritual of birth a mere formality.

All parents wish their own dreams on their children, but for you I have but the simplest list. I wish for you quiet moments when you are filled with the sudden sweep of a summer storm, empty of all thoughts, consumed with the blinding flash of light, the hiss of rain moving through the valley, the wild whipping of the birch and poplar, the silvery underside of their leaves exposed by the wind.

I wish that when you stand upon the ground, you stand firmly, rooted in place, happy to be just where you are at that moment, thinking only of your next step.

I wish for the rapture of conquering your deepest fears and the great satisfaction of hard work that is rewarded.

I wish for you hands that have felt the thick loamy soil of our valley, hands that have gripped a shovel and hoe, that have the strength to turn over the heavy, wet soil of spring to plant potatoes and corn.

I wish you the joy of rising with the sun, eager to push on with the day while others sleep.

I wish you the cool, deft hands of a baker, with a keen, light touch.

And although life will deliver blows and setbacks, I wish you the goodwill and determination to always see it through, without self-pity and with a high regard for doing the right thing.

These things I wish for you, but I can give you none of them. It is a father's great sorrow that he is but a witness, a bystander in the life of his children. But I can give you the love and comfort of this family; stories told at bedtime that have become part of our history; of mud fights up at the pond; cool evenings shucking corn on the back porch; of walks down the dirt road at night, the lantern sending out a spray of yellow light across the dusty trunks of wild apple trees.

I can only hope to give you the briefest glimpses into a world seen by just a few, those who have the patience to seek out the rich rewards of faith in the unseen. I promise you that when you are ready to stand, I will take your tiny hand in mine and we will walk together through this valley of light and darkness, the two of us seeking out the path that lies ahead.

seven

You know her as Mom

"SHE WAS THE MOST INTENSELY ALIVE
PERSON I HAD EVER MET..."

———————

This is a story about your mother in the early days, long before we had children. You know her now as Mom, the woman who picks you up at the bus stop every day at four o'clock, who gives you change to buy candy from the gum ball machine at the dry cleaners, whose voice rises to fever pitch after she has asked you a dozen times to please pick up your room, and who is always there to dispense cough syrup, Band-Aids, and chocolate milk when most needed.

For you, she is an institution, the unelected head of this great bureaucracy we call our family. She enforces the rules, metes out justice, and keeps the complex system of risks and rewards in fine tune so we don't slowly sink into domestic chaos. Most of all, she offers a great well of understanding, a deep draught of sympathy that is available to all without regard to slights and injuries visited upon her by our selfishness and lack of concern.

But this is about your mom before those days, when she was younger and more carefree, full of spunk and vinegar, her thick coils of red hair sprouting madly from her head, swinging this way and that from constant motion. She was—and still is—the most intensely alive person I had ever met, always eager, always anticipating, always ready to drive on two wheels around the next bend. She was a good letter writer, too, leaving me romantic notes where I least expected them: on car seats, under a pillow, tucked into my toilet case on a business trip. She was coltish in those days—handsome, frisky, and unpredictable. When her face produced that mischievous grin, I was never quite sure what would happen, but something unexpected and wonderful always did.

Above all, your mother is determined, unwilling to be discouraged or let a disappointing turn of events cloud her enjoyment of life. Some may call her stubborn, but I would describe her as single-minded, unwilling to drift with the odd current or be put off from the task at hand by distractions. As determined as she is to get a job done, she is also unwilling to be distracted from her love for each of you by thoughtlessness and bad behavior.

Being a good mother takes patience, a keen eye for ripples on the water, and a good nose for a change of weather. Like all parents, she is an easy target, still and unmoving, but don't be taken in by her familiarity. Beneath the surface are many things unseen, crosscurrents that rarely boil to the surface. The frisky teenager, the girlfriend, the lover, the businesswoman, and the best friend are all there in a sly glance or a moment of reflection. To miss them in your great haste to grow up is to miss the full measure of a remarkable life, one that has much to offer as you grow into each of these roles yourself.

Here, at your doorstep, is a bold passion for life, a drama performed each and every day, so when your turn comes, you will appreciate her brilliant turn on life's broad stage, making it all look so easy. Then you will realize even the slightest gestures to the audience take years of practice and the right stuff. Take my advice and learn what you can from a master. And when she brings down the house, don't forget to give her a good round of applause. Even the best of them like to play to a grateful audience.

PART TWO

Small Town, U.S.A.

eight

Bingo night at the fire station

"IT IS A GIFT TO KNOW THAT A SEAT IS
RESERVED FOR EACH OF US, THAT A HEAVENLY
HOMECOMING IS OURS FOR THE ASKING…"

—————————

*L*ast August, our family drove over to the next town, which was having its annual fireman's parade and carnival. Although it was past five, the sun was still hard at work, and we walked slowly into the main stretch of road that passes for a town center, the firehouse being the center of attraction at one end, the congregational church at the other. In front of the firehouse, hundreds of folding lawn chairs had been set up, brought by eager townspeople and visitors, the frayed bands of yellow and green tightly stretched across aluminum frames, having to support the weight of farmers grown fat on a diet of potatoes, meat, and bread.

Across the street, another hundred spectators sat, a collage of long white dresses, tank tops, gray beards, green work pants held up by suspenders, kids with freckles the size of blueberries, and solemn-faced women who looked like dowagers in the orchestra section of the opera, double-chinned and demanding a fine performance. Behind the firehouse, the food stands were open for business in whitewashed cabins, with stained counters, offering homemade fries, hot dogs, hamburgers, and fried dough. The fries were good, dumped onto dark-stained paper bags, glistening with hot oil, and then shoveled into small cardboard containers almost too hot to carry. The fried dough was slathered with melted butter and sprinkled with a thick layer of sugar and cinnamon, and eaten hot, the sugar sticking like sand to the lips and fingers. Inside a tent were games of chance, and in the hall itself, bingo cards had been laid out with dried corn kernels for markers. The board in back, where the on-duty volunteers were listed, was filled with good local names such as Morey and Truehart, Mackey and Tifft, Putnam and Zinn. I had known Morey's father, Merritt, a man who'd rather tell a story than eat supper. He used to live just down the road on the corner, right where the game wardens set up "Bambi," a remote control buck used to lure unsuspecting hunters who are arrested for shooting from a car.

Soon enough, the parade started with the fire trucks from the adjoining towns. Kids with big ears that stuck out like side-view mirrors waved from the high cabs. Locals cheered at the sight of a next-door neighbor. Small candies were thrown from the backs of trucks for the children, a spray of tightly wrapped sweets skidding across the pavement, skittering underneath ambulances and chairs. A few bands marched their way through town, wearing heavy red woolen uniforms that hung limply in the sun, sweat beading up on foreheads and then running down, pooling up over bushy eyebrows and then diverting off to the side of the face as if by a water bar. Homemade floats displayed hunting scenes, complete with pine trees, the mounted heads of bucks, two or three boys dressed in full camouflage with Black Bear bows, and always the banner advertising "The Vermont Predator" or perhaps something less bloodthirsty, such as "Hunt and Fish the Green Mountains of Vermont."

In these small towns, everyone has a place—the volunteer firemen, the sheriff, the carpenters, the selectman, the farmers, and the kids marching next to their fathers in the band. These little towns are not home to a World Series baseball team or a football stadium, nor do they have summer theater or fancy weddings. They are dusty towns, too small and too poor even for junior league. Bingo night occurs only once per year, on the day of their big parade, when firemen and trombone players and young couples with brightly waxed muscle cars slowly make their way down Main Street to the fire hall, where they are cheered and counted, where each of them is somebody in a town that nobody has much heard of.

As each of our children grows older and shakes the dust from their shoes, they will be anxious to be rid of the sight of french fries left in the dust by the ball toss and large doughy women in bright green shorts surrounded by small dirty faces. But many years from now, on a hot night in August, it will be bingo night once again, and they will hear the blast of the horn on top of the fire truck. Each of their names will be posted on the firehouse wall that evening, with the Moreys and Tiffts, the town knowing that they are willing and able to do their duty if called to action. It is a gift to know that a seat is reserved for each of us, that a heavenly homecoming is ours for the asking. We just need to stop and listen for the sound of the band on a hot night in August, calling us to sit elbow to elbow with our neighbors, asking if we are ready to accept the luck of the draw with good faith and fellowship.

nine.

A town with a past

"LISTEN TO YOUR MEMORIES AND TAKE NOTE
OF WHERE YOU HAVE BEEN..."

———————

Your grandmother, my mother, once gave me good advice about choosing a town to settle in. It should be small enough to have a sense of community, a local newspaper, and, of course, a good library. For my part, I would add that a town should have a past, a sense of history that provides shape and definition to its crossings and corners so that even a short drive down its streets offers a bit of biographical narrative.

In our small town in Vermont, I often point a finger out the window to signal where old Crofut's car ran off the road back in the 1960s, or the cellar hole where once stood the west-side Congregational Church at a time when our town had three places of worship and two dance halls. The old-timers can also point out cellar holes from the nineteenth century, when our town boasted seven schools, two stores, two sawmills, a stagecoach tavern, a gristmill, a flaxmill, and two blacksmith shops, plus an assortment of factories making clothespins, oyster barrels, brushbacks, and cheese.

Art Mears used to run a general store out of his house just across from the church, selling flour, sugar, oatmeal, kerosene, ammunition, beef, tobacco, and the like. There was another store owned by Minor Herd up in Beartown when there was a full-time logging operation run by the Wilcox family. The mill was run by steam power and they sawed squares for chair stock, which was pulled by teams fifteen miles to the next town down the main road, past the church, the store, and the town hall (which burned down twenty years ago and was rebuilt). That part of town even had a boardinghouse and dance hall for the workers. Today, none of these buildings is still standing except the Methodist church (we outlasted the Congregationalists) and the number two schoolhouse, which is no longer in use.

But our town also carries memories of events as well as buildings. Tudor Road was the place that the town bulldozer jumped out of gear and went hell-for-leather down the side of the mountain toward the main road. There's the spot by the old Hughes place where Charlie Randall caught the Hayes brothers going by on their wagon with a big jacked doe propped up between them, thinking they might fool Charlie, whose eyesight wasn't so good. And the road right in front of the church bore witness many times to our herd of pigs running free, having rooted underneath the sheep fence on the farm.

On summer nights, I like to roll down the windows and inhale a deep breath of the cool, moist air, perfumed with pine and wintergreen. It brings back memories of my sister and I holding on for dear life in the back of an old army jeep, my mother driving at full speed up the loose gravel roads after a good ration of Jim Beam. They were wild nights, the rush of the wind, the sound of the peepers and bullfrogs whistling by, all of us liberated from the tired monotony of the hot, dusty days, somehow freed by the sheer nonsense of it all. It is as if the town is awash in memories, their moorings loose, floating about the hollows and high up on the ridges, just ripe for catching, for those of us who have a mind to snare them.

But on still and moonless nights, I sometimes catch other memories as well, of things I should have done; people forgiven, blessings bestowed, actions undone. Like this small town, each of you is constructing your own past, a ledger book that totals the sum of your life here on earth. As the columns fill, you will come more clearly into focus, your future circumscribed by your past. So on a dark, breathless evening, listen to your memories and take note of where you have been. It will help you to see where you are going.

ten.

The man from Plymouth Gap

"HUMAN ENDEAVORS ARE
ROOTED IN WHAT THE LORD HAS MADE..."

---

*L*ast summer, we visited Plymouth, Vermont, the
small town where Calvin Coolidge was born. It is
situated in a narrow valley, with steep hills rising on two
sides, a country road winding past the homestead. What strikes
the first-time visitor most is the overwhelming simplicity of
the place. The eye is deeply satisfied with the flow of snow-
white clapboards, the irregular patterns of stone foundations,
the thin line of old mullions, the fun-house distortions of wavy

glass panes, and the play of light and shadow underneath large, spreading maples.

On a cool August afternoon, we stood in this small Vermont valley and, for me, it was a homecoming, the place I visit in chance dreams, arriving by horse and buggy, with the clip of horseshoes on packed dirt and the swish of tail on a chestnut rump.

It is hard to communicate the deep sense of peace that emanates from this steadfast group of buildings, from the cheese factory and the schoolhouse, from the modest garden to the homestead, from the three-story barn to the Union Christian Church. They sit on the land intentionally, designed and built with purpose and forethought, having settled into their foundations like old friends snugly ensconced in settled armchairs. The power of the land itself is palpable, like the thick scent of an old barn, taking you in, making you put down roots, the earth reaching upward through your thick-soled boots. The homestead is both a destination and a beginning, providing a good foundation for children and a place of rest and contemplation for those weary of the temporal satisfactions of modern life.

Although never given his due in the history books, there is much to learn from Calvin Coolidge, a president, a farmer, a poet, and a man of great parsimony in his speech and habits. Of his mother, who died when he was only twelve, he wrote, "It seemed as though the rich green tints of the foliage and the blossoms of the flowers came for her in the springtime, and in the autumn it was for her that the mountainsides were struck with crimson and with gold."

But he also had a keen wit and good sense of humor. During a tour of a chicken farm, his wife had gone ahead of him and noted a frisky rooster who was actively servicing a hen. She asked, "Is he always like this?" When assured that this was normal behavior, she said, "Please tell that to Mr. Coolidge." When the president started the tour, he was informed of the rooster's energetic activities, and he asked, "Does this rooster service a different hen every day?" When told that he did, Mr. Coolidge stated, "Please tell that to Mrs. Coolidge."

He loved to wear an old wool frock around the farm and large calfskin boots, both of which belonged to his grandfather. Hard work was the order of the day, living a life of frugality and obedience. There was no room for self-glory in the office of president, Coolidge understanding that most politicians waver between humble servitude in the face of greater power and gross flights of self-importance, the office itself having got the better of the man. Here was a Vermonter and a president, who stepped down after his first full term in office, declining to run again, having done his service to country and God. He knew that it was by mere happenstance that he was propelled to the highest office in the land.

Of all the presidents you study in school—from Thomas Jefferson to Abe Lincoln, from Teddy Roosevelt to John Kennedy—remember first Coolidge for his love of family and land, for his devotion to frugality and community. Above all, honor Coolidge for his devout sense of humility, for his grateful acceptance of what life has to offer. Whether it was good haying weather or the presidency, Coolidge took it in stride with a "thanks be to God."

And at Plymouth Gap, the site of his homestead, one comes to understand that human endeavors are rooted in what the Lord has made. Houses built on vanity suddenly go out of fashion, the rooms empty of furniture, left to the slow but determined effects of time and weather. Never rooted in deep soil, these structures are quickly drained of life, the cold seeping into the lathe and wallpaper, dampness settling into the floorboards. But at the Coolidge homestead, the simple lines of clapboard and humble splash of whitewash were designed not as a monument to human achievement, but as modest shelter. These walls still harbor echoes from his oath of office, taken in the front parlor, and the sound of church bells on Sunday morning. Learn from Coolidge and build your structures well but with deep humility, knowing that only the house of the Lord will last forever.

eleven

Old home day

"EACH OF US HAS A SPECIAL PLACE AT THE TABLE,
A HEAVENLY INVITATION TO PARTICIPATE
IN THE GREAT ADVENTURE OF LIFE..."

As each of you knows well, our small Methodist church celebrates Old Home Day on the first Sunday in August. It's a time for present and former members of the congregation to visit, sing hymns, and read the list of those who have passed on, their seats now vacant or taken by a visitor or a weekender, unaware of those who had filled the pews before. The minister starts the service by asking those present to call out favorite hymns by number, and then we sing two verses, always the first and usually the last.

Last summer, we began promptly at one o'clock with "Precious Lord, Take My Hand," Martin Luther King's favorite hymn and one well known by the congregation. The man in the pew just ahead of me called out "My Faith Looks Up to Me," and then we sang "Because He Lives," followed by "What a Friend We Have in Jesus," "Be Thou My Vision," and "For All the Saints." We sang well that day, voices given freely, the melody floating out across the field of alfalfa and down to the Green River to the old Baptist hole where I had gone swimming so many times as a kid.

Each of you has taken part in this simple celebration, being part of the children's singing group. Last summer, you sang "Kumbaya," each child having a small solo part. Charlie, this was your first year as one of the singers and you did us proud, shirt half-tucked in but face aglow, aware of the attention and smiles of the visitors as you stood squarely, facing the audience, gathering steam as you got to the last verse. That day it was your turn to shine, more than a few tears brought to the eyes of the congregation, as you were surrounded by leggy ten-year-olds who stood like great shafts of oak towering over a young seedling. And then the minister handed out small pins to the singers but had none for you, since you were a last-minute addition to the choir. You stood up in the pew as your sisters were moving to the front of the church and cried out desperately, "Where's mine?" In your moment of greatest triumph, you had once again been left out, not counted as part of the gang. It was all I could do to hold you back, grabbing a fistful of shirttail and then a waistband as you pulled mightily like an ox headed stubbornly to the end of the row.

But I wanted to write you about what happened after the service. It was a sunny day, warm but not hot, with a cool breeze coming in from the west. Picnic tables had been placed under the maple trees and the food had been set out under simple canopies of weathered cloth: baked beans, potato salad, olives, celery, fresh boiled corn, coleslaw, hamburgers, hot dogs, sausage, and green salad. Strangers and relatives sat together, faces dimly remembered from my childhood, a sea of Bentleys, Crofuts, Skidmores, and Wilcoxes. For them, I was still a child, a towheaded kid that was last seen on a bicycle coming back up from the barn after milking. And for you, I was a father, a man impossibly old, whose age cannot be counted on fingers.

As the breeze skiffled through the leaves and the
conversation ebbed and flowed like the sound of a small brook
muffled by a dense stand of pine, I looked up and saw each of
you eating ice cream out of narrow plastic cups with wooden
spoons. You ran out into the hayfield behind the church to
play hide-and-seek in the second crop of timothy, heads
popping up like nervous woodchucks from the fresh, green
growth. You snagged brownies from the dessert plates in the
back of the church, hiding by the old two-seater outhouse with
your ill-gotten sweets. And every so often you would drift by
our table, checking in, needing a bit of reassurance about when
we were leaving, making sure that all was stable and predictable.

On Sunday mornings in hard oak pews, we come to seek
peace, to find our place in the world, to be comforted by the
infinite grace of God. But here, at our modest picnic, we had
found grace in the shouts of children, in the pop and bite of
freshly boiled corn, in four generations of Vermonters bound
together by geography, sitting shoulder to shoulder, consoled
by well-worn stories. It was a timeless Sunday afternoon in
August when the past and the future circled each other from a
distance, one eye locked on history and one on the promise of

things yet to come. As you grow older, you will begin to sense your place in this continuum, like a pup realizing, at first bite, that the tip of his tail is indeed connected to his head. Each part is essential to the whole, your shouts and footfalls blending with the satisfied hum of conversation, the faint rustle of paper tablecloths and the short burst of knowing laughter at the end of a familiar story. As you grow older, your role will change, supplying the heavier tones of organ to the lighter strings of youth. But each of us has a special place at the table, a heavenly invitation to participate in the great adventure of life, seeking out its mysteries in the sound of leaves dancing in the stout maples just above our heads.

twelve.

Quite a character

"LIVE LIFE FOR THE PURE JOY OF IT..."

———————

*I*n our part of Vermont, country fairs still have pie-judging competitions, the competing slices of apple, blueberry, or lemon meringue pies set out on display, most of them receiving a ribbon. But it is easy to forget that fairs used to be a celebration of the harvest when the hard work was done, the hay baled and stored, the corn chopped into silage, the fields turned under for next spring's planting. Around the turn of the century, a neighboring town always had a large country fair, and Arnold Wilcox tells a story about his grandfather, Frasier Mears, who hiked over the mountain to this fair with his eighty-year-old uncle. On the way home, the uncle was tired and stopped for a nap in a cow pasture. Frasier was anxious to get back, so he picked up a small bit of cow manure and placed it in his uncle's outstretched right hand as he lay snoring on his back. Then he tickled his nose with a small piece of timothy, which had the desired effect. Frasier said he got home pretty quick that evening, his uncle chasing him all the way up and over the mountain like a man half his age.

Frasier was quite a character—and also quite a practical joker. He lived on the edge of a pasture up in the mountains and liked his privacy, so when a new family moved in just below him, he set out at night, tacked a length of violin string to the clapboards of their small house and hid in the bushes, holding the other end. Just after they went to bed, he pulled out his violin bow and played the string, making an eerie, haunted humming. After three nights, the unsuspecting couple would up and leave town.

In the old days in our town, there were lots of characters like Frasier, old-timers who didn't care a whit for what others thought of them. Most of us remember seeing Russell Baines, a metalworker, who would park his old blue station wagon by the side of the road, eat potato chips, read a romance novel, and then go to sleep. He had moved in with Charlie Bentley, a local farmer, and to get some privacy he would start up the old car every afternoon and go in search of a new place to park. Pretty soon, the whole town got used to the sight of Russell, head angled out the window, his large ears and thick, black-frame glasses visible from the road, taking his daily nap, peaceful in his own car.

Another character was Merritt Morey. He liked to tell the story of the new teacher at the one-room schoolhouse across from the church. Merritt noticed that she used to visit the outhouse just before ringing the bell for school, so he got to school early one winter day and nailed the door shut. She was forced to go in a snowbank and never came back. Another year, a new teacher showed up one day and, since she didn't lay down the law in terms of behavior, Merritt thought things were going to be pretty easy. Well, he tore off a small piece of hard rubber ball and tossed it on top of the wood stove. Before long, it got to smoking and stinking up the classroom. The teacher got up, walked over to the stove, flicked off the burning rubber, and then walked casually past Merritt's desk. The next thing he knew he was flat on his back on the floor, the side of his face starting to swell from a good solid whack from the back of her hand. She asked if anyone else was interested in a bit of the same, and things ran pretty well after that.

These days, the Frasiers or Merritts are curiously scarce, like the bobcats that used to live up on the rocky ridge behind the farm. Heed the old stories and become a character yourself. Throw your hat in the air and let out a whoop when you're feeling good. Jump on a horse backward just because you've never done it before. Follow a swarm of bees all day just to see where they hole up. Live life for the pure joy of it and let others stand by the side of the road, watching you gallop by, holding on for dear life.

thirteen.

The road out of town

"WE WILL BE SAD TO SEE YOU DRIVE
OUT OF THE VALLEY, BUT EVERY JOURNEY
MUST HAVE A BEGINNING..."

Our town has but three main roads: one is the main
road up to Beartown, another veers off to the west
through the notch (a narrow mountain pass) and down into
the valley where we have our farm, and the third goes pretty
much east, up over a four-wheel-drive track, down into the
next village. Many are named after old town families, such as
Wilcox or Woodcock. They wind through the hollows or
around the hills and mountains that ring with a small-town
accent, Swearing Hill and Minister Hill, which face each other

across the valley, or Red, Moffitt, and Bear Mountains, which rise to just over three thousand feet.

Our town is also blessed with many small streams, most of which feed into the Green River, including Terry Brook, Chunks Creek, and Baldwin Brook over on the west side, and Pruddy Brook, Hopper Brook, and Tidd Brook in the main part of town. I used to live nearby Tidd Brook as a child, catching small crawfish and trout under the barn-red wooden bridge. The sound of the cars rattling the old timbers, one at a time, echoed off the side hills of our small hollow, but today they are just a memory now that the bridge has been replaced by a cheaper and quieter culvert.

Back then, there weren't many cars on our roads and they moved slowly, old Charlie Bentley Sr. hunched over the large steering wheel of a black 1950 Ford or Fred Woodcock Sr. driving down to the row of mailboxes, anxious for his Social Security check. As each car worked its way across the stream, each board had time to move up and down, forward and backward in its place, the hollow thumping always in the same key but playing a song with different notes. In bed at the end of a long summer day, I would stare out my window at the side hill of thistle and timothy and wait for the sound of a crossing, for a sign of movement in the still, hot air, a promise of a chance visit to break the silence of the house.

Country life is blessed with lazy drifts of silence, vast stretches of time when the house starts to cool on a summer evening, the dishes washed and put away, the hectic pace of the day ebbing in the twilight. It is then that I hear the rhythmic creak of the rope on the swing set, the muffled report of backgammon pieces snapped onto the thick padded board, the snuffling and gulping of little Emily at her mother's breast, finally settling down to dinner. A dog barks down by the old Lincoln place or we hear two bears high up on ridges, hooting to one another across the valley.

But it is our dusty country road that most often brings us sounds from the outside world—the throaty roar of a backhoe slowly making its way into town or the steady, determined popping of rubber on gravel as a pickup works its way down from the notch toward the broad, flat valley below. Like good Vermonters, we often sit on the front porch as the sun slips behind Egg Mountain, the colors draining out of our vista, the valley flat, distances compressed by the waning light. And your mother and I think about that old road that runs by our house. Like Baldwin Brook in April, it will widen its banks, sweeping away each of you in turn, taking you out of our valley and into foreign currents that are deep and laden with peril. It seems to me that this road is connected to all things in the outside world. It runs over to New York State and then down to the city or out into the vast plains of the West and then perhaps on to the Pacific.

Yet it is a good thing to get in the old red pickup and start down the road in any direction you choose. The view from the front porch will not suit you for a lifetime. We will be sad to see your taillights wink off and on between the sugar maples as you drive out of the valley, but your mother and I know that every journey must have a beginning.

fourteen.

Walking down
a country road

"THERE ARE TIMES WHEN IT IS
A GOOD THING TO BE WITHOUT DESTINATION…"

On summer evenings after dinner, the six of us take a walk down the country road that winds in front of our farm. I hoist Charlie onto my shoulders, put little Emily on my hip, or perhaps hold hands with Whitney and Caroline, slowly walking down to Baldwin Brook, past the corn and potato fields, and then up past the row of apple trees and then down to the horse barn and henhouse just below our neighbor's. In late June, the timothy is high in our lower field, ripe for cutting and baling, the tops about to burst with seed. In the twilight, the row of white beehives at the other end of this field are half obscured by the tall grass, the stacked boxes dimly lit in the half-light. There are no cars now, but the still evening air is filled with other sounds—the gurgle of the brook, the whippoorwill and chirrup of evening bird songs, the low neigh of a workhorse in an upper field, and the frantic rustle of a chipmunk in the tall grass as we walk by.

I look about and see our small family surrounded by a handsome bowl of trees and old clapboard farmhouses, underneath a great canopy of peach and copper sky, the thickening colors the only measure of passing time. We see a row of white birches standing to attention at the edge of a meadow, holding back the encroaching forest. A dead gray oak stands naked above a copse of black birch and poplar, childlike in its sticklike parsimony. A narrow brook meanders through the valley dressed prettily in a wrap of leafy brush, putting the freshly-mown pasture to shame.

This is our happiest hour as a family, walking down a country road on a full stomach, looking forward on our return to a thick slice of cold strawberry rhubarb pie or a fresh scoop of blueberry cobbler served in a custard-colored bowl, topped with a generous splash of thick cream. It is a time for horseplay, Whitney or Caroline jumping up behind me, trying to hijack a piggyback ride, or Charlie, running in circles, chatting on about cowboys. We have no destination. We might walk for five minutes or fifty. We might meet a neighbor and stay to chat, or wave and keep going. We might turn off the road and hike up into the west-side cemetery, playing hide-and-seek amidst the tombstones, stopping every so often to read an epitaph we've overlooked before.

On this night, as the sky deepens and the colors shift from peach to plum, the light draining from the fields, the mountains losing shape as they are no longer framed against a backdrop of illuminated sky, we have no purpose. There are times when it is a good thing to be without destination, for it is then that we often discover where we really wish to go.

fifteen

The country store

"EACH OF US NEEDS TO LIVE
ON A CONTINUUM, WITH ONE FOOT
IN THE PAST AND ONE IN THE FUTURE…"

O n summer evenings when I was ten years old, Charlie Bentley and I would drive down to the country store after milking, with Dixie, his high-strung collie, nervously dripping saliva onto the dark green seat, one leg balanced painfully on my thigh. I can still smell the manure on my boots, the pile of baling twine, pliers, and Bag Balm sitting precariously on the dashboard and the feel of Dixie's hot breath in my ear. As soon as the truck rolled to a stop, I'd jump down from the high cab, eager for a cream soda and a package of

Mallo Cups, rounds of milk chocolate mixed with crispy coconut and filled with marshmallow.

In those days, the store was smaller, part of the house still occupied by the owners. But, like today, it was a real working-man's hangout, not a tourist destination. The old store had everything, and I remember sorting through stacks of duct and masking tape, road flares, Tung-Sol auto lamps, and Goof-off paint remover, as well as boxes of ammunition, everything from .22 shorts to .12-gauge shotgun shells for dove and quail (number 8 shot), rabbit and squirrel (number 6), and pheasant (number 4). Later, when I took up fishing, I chose among the Umpqua flies, including a Gray Yellow Hackle, an Elk Caddis, and a Trico Spinner.

But it was the toys that I loved the most. Today, the store keeps a good assortment, and I watch each of you disappear down the row, admiring Hacky Sack Footbags, Wolf Pack Bang Snaps, Assorted Color Smoke Bombs, Tippy Toes Finger Puppets, Jetfire Gliders, a jumbo bag of My Farm Animals with 16 pieces, an Explorer H2O Rocket, a Woody Woodpecker Magic Draw, removable tattoos, Giant Outdoor Chalk, and a Bible Song Singalong. My favorites were the box of Black Snake fire tablets, the cap guns, and the green plastic water pistol that would last only 24 hours, the trigger hanging loose from the fingerguard after just a few fill-ups. For candy, you try to decide between bags of jelly beans, gumdrops, candy watches, and the original hard-chew Bazooka Joe bubble gum.

Today, I am sitting on the porch of this old store with a can of Dr Pepper, watching the cheap American flag flutter occasionally in the hot breeze, listening to the clank of the cowbell and excited voices as you flit from one attraction to the next, trying to decide between candy lipstick and bubble gum tape or the small yellow plastic bank and the miniature finger puppets. More than any other place I know, this narrow porch is a place of comfort, sagging a bit under the weight of time and customers, but unchanged to my eye, offering a clear view of history.

I suspect that each of us needs to live on a continuum, with one foot in the past and one in the future, and this is my spot to view it clearly. I can see old Charlie Bentley Sr. drive up in his black Ford and Fred Woodcock making a trip down to the store for a can or two of Genessee. But I can also see you, Charlie, or perhaps Caroline, sitting where I am now, ears tuned to your children inside and eyes searching the length of this tired road, seeking a memory of a hot summer afternoon, an old pickup, and a father who was still young and unbowed from the passage of time.

PART THREE

Simple Pleasures

sixteen.

A cool glass of water

"WHEN WE ARE TRULY
AT PEACE, HAPPINESS BUBBLES UP
TO THE SURFACE LIKE COOL SPRING WATER..."

This last week has been hot in Vermont, the temperature reaching the high nineties, the back porch floodlit by a hot sun by 6:00 A.M., the kitchen no longer cool in the early morning hours but heavy and humid, having been unable to exhale the heat and bustle of the previous day. On these dog days of summer, one aches for a fresh start, for a cool breeze to gently introduce the new day, for a brisk, fresh wind from the east to dry our sweat-soaked shirts and cool our foreheads when we tip our caps to the change in weather. Even a dip in the pond is no longer refreshing, since the water is bathtub warm, with only occasional spouts of cool undercurrents bubbling up from hidden springs.

But our farm still has one great pleasure—a tall glass of well water gulped down between chores, cool but not ice-cold, a burst of refreshment that is unequaled in all of the great cuisines of the world. I would rather stand at the kitchen sink on a hot July day, drinking a tall glass from this underground current than dine at the greatest four-star eateries of Paris, feasting on perfectly sautéed foie gras with a touch of vinegar or perhaps a confit of duck served in a small bistro with a cheap but honest glass of red wine.

These simple pleasures are there for the taking. Sitting on the front porch, I watch each of you roll down the grassy hill to the swing set, giggling and shouting, like a rollicking stampede of human logs. Or you set off into the brush on an overcast day, in search of a bright orange salamander, hidden under a rock or near a small stream. Or you veer off our dirt driveway into the undergrowth, searching for a secret patch of raspberries and come back wide-eyed with a chance encounter with a young buck, who snorted at you from a nearby stand of trees, his small sprout of horns just noticeable in the late afternoon light. And you make up games, shouting out rules that change by the second, scampering about setting boundaries, Charlie high on the thrill of being old enough to participate with his two older sisters. Or I find you, Caroline, seated outside, back straight in the fading evening light, knitting away, making a small present for your father, which is received with great ceremony and love. Or Whitney, you set off at twilight with shovel in hand to dig new potatoes for dinner, returning with more small red spuds than we can eat in a week.

These pleasures are what summers are made for—shedding time and entertainments, avoiding deadlines and conflicts, expanding days until they have no end, filled with simple amusements. When we are truly at peace, time stops and happiness bubbles up to the surface like cool spring water. Like good Vermonters, we should have the common sense to stand by the sink when we are thirsty, heads tilted upward, drinking to our contentment, knowing that even on the hottest day of the year, there is always a cool glass of water if we know where to look for it.

seventeen.

At the Dairy Bar

"As you make your own way
in this world, be comforted that
you can find paradise wherever you look for it..."

———————

We stopped one perfect Saturday afternoon at
Shaw's Dairy Bar, each of you begging for a soft-
serve ice cream cone. It's a small establishment just south of
town, with a menu that offers its own special shorthand. There
were Wing Zings, kielbasa with kraut, meatball grinders, foot-
long dogs, barnburgers, corn dogs, Michigan dogs, cheese
sticks, buckets of chicken, and onion rings. But you were there
for dessert, perhaps a Frozen Eat-It-All Sandwich or a Slush
Puppy or the soft-serve ice cream that comes in eight different

flavors, including banana ripple. You could order chocolate, rainbow, or krunch-kote sprinkles on top, but I knew you would go for a big cone of the bubble gum ice cream, swirled with pink flavoring on a stocky cone. Your mother remembers the original bubble gum ice cream with real pieces of Bazooka in it. The trick was not to eat any of the cone since it stuck to the gum, which otherwise could be chewed and blown after the ice cream was finished.

Built onto the side of the Dairy Bar is a small shed called the dining area with red painted benches lining the inside walls. Three smirking teenage boys were sitting there, waiting patiently for something to happen, talking with a bit more animation than was called for by the content of their conversation. Napkins stained with the bloodred of ketchup and smears of chocolate ice cream sprang fitfully across the well-worn grass in the lively breeze. Whole families sat in vans in the parking area, licking and sucking swirled towers of freshly exuded confection. Pickups and motorcycles passed by but without the intensity of destination, just out for the ride.

And our family sat at one of the tables, tongues extended, licking great furrows in the velvety soft-serve—cool, creamy gobs sliding slowly across the tongue and then continuing deliciously toward the back of the throat. Then I began to notice the play of the branches in the large oak nearby, the breeze a fine thing on a hot summer afternoon. I looked at the people around us. An older couple was seated at a picnic table, the man's bright tortoiseshell glasses framed in stark relief by his nearly bald and perfectly round, close-cropped head. His features were small and simple, his expression entirely focused on the matter at hand, staring at a partially eaten onion ring, the milky white insides pulled halfway out of the crisp brown ring on the first bite. Other folks appeared whitewashed and crazed by the end of winter, the sort of strangers one might avoid in the supermarket checkout or down at the country store; old bachelors who talk maliciously about their neighbors and women who stop washing their hair, their dark tresses limp and stringy. But on this day, everyone looked reborn. An unkind thought or a slight tic at the corners of the mouth had been forgiven by the warmth of the sun and the childlike pleasure of the Dairy Bar.

As you make your own way in this world, be comforted that you can find paradise wherever you look for it—in a napkin skittering across a well-worn lawn, in the summer's first bite of ice cream, or in the face of a stranger transformed by the power of God's grace on a summer's day.

eighteen.

To take a sauna

"EACH OF US CAN BE RELEASED FROM THAT SMALL DARK ROOM OF OUR OWN MAKING AS SOON AS WE ARE WILLING TO STAND UP AND TAKE THE PLUNGE..."

———————

Many of the Vermonters in our small town are of Finnish descent and so the woods and backyards are dotted with small one-story structures. These are saunas of various shapes and condition, many now abandoned and grown over with vine and stinging nettle. Your grandmother was no exception, having thrown together a tiny house of rough-sawn pine, benches assembled with hammers and sixteenpenny nails, the roof made from plywood and cheap gray barn shingles. I drove by it last summer and was sad to see that it had sunk into the brush by Tidd Brook, deflated now, old memories of sweat and candlelight having fled its rotten walls.

Just this summer, we built our own family sauna, a two-story bit of whimsy with a steep, angled roof, dormers, and a good cedar-lined sauna room. It has a narrow porch out front with two benches where we can sit and look out over the Green Mountains, the sauna sitting up high on the edge of a meadow, just a few feet from our small pond.

After a few test fires to burn off any extra stove black, we settled in for our first family sauna. The stove had been preheated for over an hour, the air whistling through the front grate, the wood popping, the stove creaking from the intense heat. The cedar planks were warmed, a subtle incense of resin and forest emanating into the close room. I lit a hanging candle and three of you marched in with your mother, little three-month-old Emily left just outside in the dressing room, asleep and bundled in her portable rocker. At first, it was all giggles and jostling, the experience new and exciting. As the twilight ebbed and the view from the two small windows slowly faded, the dark outline of the woods beyond the upper field melted into darkness. Soon the conversation slowed and the low roar of the fire rose in our consciousness, the sweat beading on our foreheads and starting to form thin rivulets behind our ears that tickled as it ran. The heat itself became a visitor, shrouding us in its thick blanket, penetrating our lungs, softly carrying us into the night.

As the candle flickered weakly, the wax melting in the heat, we cut our tethers and went out to sea, our small family adrift in a lifeboat of the night, the current carrying us past unknown shores, our keel passing over depths charted only by the imagination. Here we were, bound in our passage by the heat and four walls, faces showing weakly in the sweltering gloom, thrown together like strangers seeking refuge and salvation. And then, just when we were about to sink into the deep, we bolted for freedom and streaked down to the pond, launching ourselves outstretched, horizontal to the cold mountain water. We plunged deep into a revelation of liquid ice and were borne up to the surface, drawn skyward by breath and momentum. Looking back, I saw the red glow from the carriage lantern on the porch, a beacon that fell across the water like the port light from a small ship. Heads bobbed, weightless and free from the pull of torso, and the sound of splashes lifted up above the pond and then out over the valley.

As we floated out among the evening stars of heaven's jubilee, I thought that each of us can be released from that small dark room of our own making as soon as we are willing to stand up and take the plunge, a country baptism of amazing grace and redemption.

nineteen.

Summer storm

"OUR SINS HAD BEEN
FORGIVEN, ABSOLVED BY THE CLEANSING RAIN..."

I remember one Thursday evening last summer when the family was sitting on our front porch after dinner, sunlight ebbing, twilight casting its gray cloak over our valley. Across the road and up above the pasture toward Egg Mountain, we watched a vast broadside of storm clouds sailing in. These were not the puffy thunderheads of daytime, but a great bank of gunmetal gray, like the bow of an enormous tanker looming up out of the darkness. The clouds were so intensely dark that we could not take our eyes off of them, expecting Zeus himself to suddenly emerge, swooping down the mountainside to blasts of thunder and jagged bolts.

The air was still and compressed, as if weighted by the clouds. Only a few birds were calling, but those still active were in sharp relief to the silence. In the half-light, the mountains across the valley were soft in appearance, the trees muted and two-dimensional, all of the form and knobby thrusts taken out of the peaks and hills. It was an expectant time—the valley held its breath, waiting for the storm to roll down the pastures and through our small basin of trees, streams, and farmhouses.

On the porch, each of you were transfixed, peering out over the high bush cranberries, over our lower field, and then up to the bank of deep charcoal clouds. The rocking chairs were large and each of you was small, hunkered down into the seat, the rockers still as the evening. We didn't speak as we watched the storm advance toward our house, imperceptibly at first, and then gathering speed as it floated past the tops of the mountains, sailing out across the sky that spreads over our valley. It was a time of waiting, of expectation, of holding one's breath, the impending storm having replaced all else on the horizon.

Then it started. The peaks across the valley were lost in the clouds, and a wall of water could be seen marching down the upper pastures. As it came closer, we could hear the hissing of the rain as it flowed down into the valley, sweeping aside the quiet, increasing in volume like a tandem trailer moving toward us down a highway. The curtain of rain swept across our hayfield and up to the house, whipping the limbs of our sugar maples into a frenzy. And then it hit. The rain pounded on the porch roof, a mad, deafening beating, the family caught in a vortex of sound and water and then crashing thunder and bursts of light. We hopped off the chairs and stepped back deeper into the porch, as the rain flowed horizontally now, waves of hard, cold pellets strafing the railing and the gray floorboards. We were huddled together by the front door for a moment, enchanted and absorbed by the power of the storm, and then went inside, the spell broken.

After you were all in bed, I stepped out into the night, the air fresh and sparkling. The rain had passed, the thunder now a distant shot of artillery in the next valley. The night was electric; the bright scent of fern, the distinct chirp of a cricket, the rustle of leaves across the valley raced by the porch as if skidding on a glassy pond, slick and smooth after a thaw and hard freeze. The past had been swept away, the hard rain had washed the decks clean, the scuppers running with clear, cold rainwater. I felt that our sins had been forgiven, absolved by the cleansing rain. Sweet forgiveness had visited our farmhouse and was visible in small faces tucked into pillowy sleep, dreamy landscapes of peace and renewal.

twenty.

Tastes both simple and sublime

"The universe is waiting for us
just outside the back door..."

———————————

Many years ago, I was helping Junior Bentley during haying season. After filling up the wagon in a small field down by the Batten Kill, he stopped the tractor and asked me to join him for a walk. We hiked down the dusty river road until we came to a spring running down a shale embankment. We cupped our hands, filling them with water that was stony cool and flinty, with a sweet aftertaste of fern and mint. He eased his cap back from his pale forehead, as white as the belly of a brook trout, and said, "Good water."

I know that farmer is familiar with every spring and brook in town, and this is his favorite. After sixty years of sipping the local waters, his palate is fine-tuned to the subtle differences between the spring by Gene Kennedy's up in Beartown and the taste of the Green River by the old Baptist hole behind the Methodist church. And on that hot day, the first sip of spring water was more refreshing than any Sancerre and sweeter than the best glass of Tokay.

It reminded me of Caroline biting into the first ear of sweet corn in early August, the kernels of silver queen just turning ripe and popping in her mouth with a burst of liquid sugar. And Whitney, you running to the potato field in mid-July with a small shovel and a bucket, digging the small red new potatoes out of the ground, then rushing back up to the house so that your dad can steam them, serving them with Jersey butter and a handful of snipped chives. As you forked them quickly into your mouth, eyes half-closed with anticipation and pleasure, I imagined you could taste the rich loam in the firm waxy spuds, alive with the clear taste of spring rains and warm summer afternoons.

I recalled the whole family hiking up to the ridge behind the house in mid-August, using old stone walls for markers, searching for the abandoned barns in the overgrown sheep meadow. There, we spent the better part of an afternoon filling one-gallon freezer bags with ripe blackberries, popping the better specimens into our mouths, our fingers becoming sticky and pricked by thorns. It was there, high up in the mountains, that a hawk swooped down from its nest or soared in lazy circles, each wing feather distinct in the clear New England light. Far away from civilization, we sat on a stone wall and rested, on top of the world, listening to a squirrel scurry through leafy branches or the sound of the wind caressing the white birch and poplar. I tasted a perfectly ripe berry, still warm from the sun. I savored its simple flavor, clear and certain, like knowing the difference between right and wrong.

In an age of ambiguity, it is comforting to find certainty in the taste of water from a country spring or in the season's first new potato. It reminds us that there is truth in the familiar, that we don't have to drive to the next town for revelations. The universe is waiting for us just outside the back door.

twenty-one.

The things I love

"WHAT I LOVE MOST IS THE
JOURNEY ITSELF..."

_____

hen I was a kid in the summer, hair bleached
white from the sun, I used to love a trip to the
country store for a grape soda, the shelves stuffed with penny
candy, balsa airplanes, and colorful boxes of harmless fireworks.
Inside the old roadside store, the air was cool and smelled of
cold cuts, stale beer, and ripe hay. I loved to come home after
milking, throwing off my clothes as I ran down the path to the
pond, plunging into the crystal-clear water that stopped my
breath for a second or two. Most of all, I loved walking the
mountains with my .22 in hand, discovering old cellar holes and

hunting camps, as I stalked grouse or rabbits, finding instead peace of mind as I moved through a stand of birches or came across a spring, bubbling up amidst a circle of fern.

Those quiet moments of my childhood are rare now that your mom and I have the four of you. The house is dense with the sound of pounding feet and plaintive shouts in the night, bedroom doors shut against the sudden cries of dark dreams. And there is the pleading, wheedling, and constantly shifting balance of power between two adults and four children—not to mention the false cries of disappointment and sticky hands placed on old velvet. But as a father, I love bending down so that you, Charlie, can whisper in my ear. I love the rare glimpse of tenderness and vulnerability that I see on your face, Whitney, when you stand unguarded and at ease. I love a hug from you, Caroline, always warm like a good parlor stove, attracting company and fellowship. I love the startled look on young Emily's face, hair standing straight in wispy thatches, eyes wide and mouth agape, when she finishes feeding, satisfied and curious. I love a hot July afternoon, hanging on to an inflatable raft in our pond, all of you stacked on top of me, trying to flip me over into the cool, green water.

And I have even come to love a child's face when it is watered by disappointment, a reservoir of tears streaking the soft, round cheeks.

I love the sound of the house before breakfast in the summer, the whirring of fans and the muted symphony of crickets' good company in the pale light. I love gently stirring batter for cornbread or muffins, pouring its thick folds into well-buttered nests for baking. I love the padded footfalls, as an early riser leaves her bed and shuffles downstairs, hair tousled and eyes thick with sleep and half-remembered dreams. And then the house awakens, the family reassembles itself for another day, old patterns and new emerging from the constant interplay of personalities.

Perhaps what I love most is the journey itself, the chance pairing of temperament and ego that we call a family. It is often heavy lifting between the cradle and the driver's seat, but while it lasts, your mother and I are at the center of the universe, here in the early morning hours, with a cup of black tea and an ear for the first step of a bare foot on Vermont hardwood.

PART FOUR

Lessons Learned

twenty-two

On working

"I WATCH AS YOU EXPERIENCE THE JOY OF LABOR,
A LESSON THAT ONCE LEARNED,
PAYS DIVIDENDS FOR A LIFETIME..."

During my childhood and now with all of you, my own kids, I have noticed that life on a farm has a peculiar charm. Work becomes pleasurable. Even young children find more excitement in feeding goats or planting seed than they do in store-bought games. Unlike most of my friends, I spent my summers milking, haying, shoveling manure, and mending fences. I found it vastly more satisfying than summers at camp or the beach. As a Maine farmer and writer, Henry Beston, once put it, there is something fine about family labor. It builds reserves of intimacy and cooperation which get us through leaner times when the sounds of the whole family at work are only sustaining memories.

In the old days, of course, kids were required to work a lot harder than you do today. The day might have started around five o'clock with the wood cooking stove being fired up. Then chores would begin, including milking cows and feeding the horses and chickens. Wood might be cut with a buck saw, and by the time a boy was fourteen or so, he would be required to work a team of horses in the field. Quite often kids were brought up in households without fathers, just uncles or grandfathers, and healthy children were important to the well-being and even survival of the family.

But for most of us these days, cooking is perhaps our last opportunity to work together as a family, each member doing his or her own vital part. I watch you, Whitney and Caroline, shucking corn, snapping beans, or whisking eggs, and I see human beings just starting out in life, discovering how far their skills can take them. And I watch as you experience the joy of labor, a lesson that once learned, pays dividends for a lifetime. You are wide-eyed with the discovery of beginnings, being witness to how flour, water, salt, and yeast rise into a thick, country loaf or an elegant twist of dinner roll. The origins of things advertise their essential mysteries without explaining them. The action of yeast is never fully understood, but once made from scratch, a loaf of bread is no longer just a product—it is a bit of the enigma of life right in our own breadbox.

These beginnings, these links to the cycle of life, are as essential to the cook as to the farmer. A good farmer must know about birthing and planting as a good cook must know how to cut up a chicken or make a starter for bread. To eat the stew without knowing its parts thins the full measure of experience. And to cook or farm by oneself is to ignore the great blessings bestowed by the community. It is a joy that reaffirms our faith in the human spirit when it is shared with others, side by side, many hands busy with common purpose.

So, remember those dark Sunday mornings, rolling out the doughnuts, cutting the rounds, gingerly slipping them into the hot fat, where they soon bobbed to the surface, speckled brown, and were quickly turned over to cook evenly. Remember the scent of freshly grated nutmeg and taste of a hot doughnut, moist, rich, clinging to the roof of your mouth, the warm vapor filling your nose as you ate. Remember the feel of your small hands on the raw dough and how you stood on the garbage can, pushing the cutter through the dough onto the counter.

We made these thick, bloated orbs of hot cooked dough together on Sunday mornings and then took them to church in a large basket lined with checkered kitchen towels. It was work, but honest labor and enjoyed by all. I give this recipe to you, the lesson of hard work followed by real satisfaction. It is a simple recipe, one that needs little instruction, but when committed to memory, it will serve you for all your life. And I also give you the memories of that small kitchen, filled with children and dough and good country smells. And when you need it the most, sit back and recall those cold, dark mornings, the kitchen alive with the bustle of hard work and fresh doughnuts.

twenty-three.

Taking your time

"IN OUR HASTE, WE MISS THE FACES
OF ANGELS HIDDEN IN THE BRUSH
AT THE EDGE OF THE WOODS..."

---

loyd Bentley was a Vermonter who never did
anything quickly. He lived in the home of Marie Briggs,
the town baker, a weathered yellow farmhouse just over the
town line from Arlington. As a kid, I'd swing open the battered
screen door and rush breathless into the dark front room—and
there would be Floyd, quietly hunched over in the shadows,
elbows on his knees, a lit cigarette in his hand. He'd look up at
me with rheumy eyes and never utter the first word. When he
did get around to saying something, it took time. It was like

watching him take a slow backswing with a bale of hay, just to start some momentum before hefting it up onto the wagon.

In those days, Floyd still mowed hay with a team of horses, making them turn on a dime with an offhand flick of the reins and a word or two uttered in the very back of the throat, almost below the range of human hearing. Mowing was slow work—I can still hear the lazy clicking of the metal gears—but that suited Floyd just fine. He was not susceptible to quick movements or fancy ideas. Slow work was honest work.

Back then, cooking was slow work, too. The kitchen in the yellow farmhouse also served as the dining room and living room. There was a faded green sofa where Floyd used to hunker down and tell stories or simply remain silent if he had nothing to say. The sink had no running water, just a hand pump. The dining table was covered with a red-and-white checkered oilcloth, which was in use all day either for eating, kneading bread, or preparing dinner. It was a busy room, never empty of visitors at any hour, really the town center for many decades. It is quiet now, although I remember the stories told in the small parlor, tales that filled the room with a special cadence, a flash of wit, a drawn-out adjective that spoke to the uncertainties of country living.

Perhaps I remember most fondly the smell of that small parlor, the ripe scent of yeast, molasses, fresh bread, green wood, wood smoke, and pickled meats, a heady perfume that seeped into the wallpaper and floorboards and that remains today. A dark, still room even in summer, its closed windows were often steamed from the simmering water on the stove. It was a world submersed in half-light, visitors appearing suddenly from the outside without warning, the sun at their backs, their approach having gone unnoticed.

It was in the small kitchen that I learned a good deal about taking one's time. The roast was started early in the morning for midday dinner and was cooked over very low heat, usually in the woodstove. We had the time for a slow-cooked roast since there was always somebody around to check on it. Corn was shucked and peas were shelled slowly—the corn while sitting on the small side porch and the peas done right at the kitchen table, Marie deftly opening the small pods while giving instructions to whomever was helping out with the dinner. A long strip of translucent brown flypaper hung from a red thumbtack in the ceiling, the muted buzzing a constant companion, like the hum of a television that gives comfort to a lonely housewife. The overstuffed mongrel, Bonnie, usually found a spot next to the woodstove and then rarely moved, the process of elevating herself to a standing position having to be considered for some minutes before being acted upon. And as is the custom in New England farmhouses, conversation, even in a crowded room, was not to be taken for granted. Long minutes might pass before someone figured they had something worth saying. In those lulls, the sound of cars passing, the murmur of boiling water, and the scratch of a dog's nails on linoleum stood out, framed by time passing slowly.

Now that I am a father, I have other memories of inaction, of the small lulls in life that carry so much weight....

Waiting for the school bus with the two of you, Whitney and Caroline, backs to the wind, faces poking out of hooded parkas or trimmed by thick blue woolen hats. The three of us were expectant at that bus stop, but also stymied by the forced wait, making small talk to pass the time or hunching over during a strong gust.

Lying in bed with my three oldest kids, about to tell a story, the mattress alive with the twitching and nuzzling of youth.

The whole family sitting in armchairs in the twilight, books put aside, staring out of the great bank of windows at an incoming storm, the trees frantic and blustery, the rain moving up the valley like a smoky curtain. For a brief moment we suspend time and action in favor of inaction. We come to recognize the benefits of doing nothing in favor of doing something just to fill time.

In our haste, we miss the faces of angels hidden in the brush at the edge of the woods or the sight of the first bluebird coming home to the small wooden house set out by the herb garden. These small things, often unnoticed, will fill your cup over time, good silage for dark winters.

The last time I saw Floyd was in the summer of 1968. His lungs were bad from the smoking, but contrary to expectations, he had made it through another winter. It was the last day of summer vacation and I had stopped by the yellow farmhouse for what turned out to be a final farewell. It was midday, almost time for dinner, and Floyd was bent over on the dull-green sofa with a cigarette. He looked up and didn't say much. He didn't have to. I knew he was busy taking his time.

twenty-four.

"Stand up, your father's passin'"

"IT IS IMPORTANT TO REMEMBER
THAT THE DETAILS MATTER, THAT IT
ALL CAN ADD UP TO SOMETHING AFTER ALL..."

———————

A few years back, your mother and I received a call from a Vermont neighbor, Jean, who said, "The fourth squirrel is in the freezer. See you Saturday night." For months, I had seen her hunkered down by the chicken coop at the side of the road with a .22 rifle loosely held across her lap. When queried about her objective, she admitted to a keen interest in squirrel hunting. But after bagging three fat specimens (gray squirrels, not the smaller, gamier red squirrels), the local population had been sufficiently decimated so that it took three months to bag the fourth and final quarry. As I soon found out, all of this small game hunting was in preparation for dinner—the classic American dish, Brunswick stew, which is made from fresh lima beans, corn, tomatoes, onions, toasted bread crumbs, and, of course, squirrel.

Besides bagging the required number of squirrel (one per person), Jean had to skin them and found instructions in the *Joy of Cooking*. (Cut through the tail bone, make cuts in the back, turn the squirrel over, and stepping on the base of the tail, pull on the hind legs until the skin comes free.) All of this took some time—the hunting, the skinning, the boning, and the actual cooking. Being thrifty and keenly devoted to living off the land, however, this was perfectly natural for Jean; as normal as grilling a couple of T-bones on the backyard grill.

When that Saturday night arrived, the four of us (Charlie and Emily were still just possibilities) walked down our driveway, past our lower field where we often pick wildflowers, including three of our favorites—joe-pye weed, butter-and-eggs, and queen of the meadow. We headed across the dirt road past a few grazing sheep and then up the hilly path to her house, a white clapboard farmhouse perched on top of a steep embankment that leads down to a small barn and chicken coop.

Inside, the house was still with the simplicity of a true Vermont home. The dining room had a wide-plank wooden floor painted gray and partially covered with a braided rug made by her mother, Dorothy, who passed away when you older girls were very young. There were no curtains—the windows opened onto a vast field of alfalfa framed by mountains—and the table was simply set with a small glass dish of bread-and-butter pickles, ironstone china, an antique castor, and two beeswax candles. Just before dinner was served, there was a brief moment of silence that captured the essence of one Vermont cook, a unique blend of frugality and plain living, that was defined by the food, the room, the view—as if all the details of her daily life had been perfectly arranged in one posed snapshot.

After a second helping of stew, a simple salad of spinach and wild leek, and a thick slice of coconut cake, it occurred to me that few of us are blessed with such a moment when everything we stand for as individuals comes together in a confluence of place and time. It is no wonder that great cooks are consistent in outlook and deeply devoted to their culinary views. Whether it is simple country cooking or the finest white-tablecloth fare, the best of us have our moment, an instant in time when a picture of our lives emerges clearly, fully developed for all to see.

As in the kitchen, when all of the small details and all the decisions we make when preparing food finally add up to a whole meal, I sometimes wonder if the same isn't true about a life well lived. If we are true to ourselves, the moment finally comes when we emerge clearly from the consuming back and forth of just getting by. I remember such a moment from *To Kill a Mockingbird*, when Atticus Finch, whose client was a hardworking black man accused of raping a local white girl, had just heard the guilty verdict given by an all-white jury.

At that moment, the spectators in the balcony rose in silence to honor a man who had risked everything—including the lives of his children—to defend a neighbor who could find no other champion. As Atticus walked down the center aisle of the courtroom toward home, Reverend Sykes took hold of Atticus's daughter Scout and whispered, "Miss Jean Louise, stand up. Your father's passin'." As a grown woman, Scout recalled that moment as the instant when her father's life came into clear focus, when all the difficult day-to-day decisions added up to a man who transcended the tired old town of Maycomb one hot summer.

It is important to remember that the details matter, that it all can add up to something after all. When each of you becomes a parent, the thought of a neighbor taking your child in hand and saying, "Stand up, your father's passin'," is perhaps more than you can hope for, but it is no more than you should expect of yourself.

twenty-five

Taciturn tutor

"GOOD TEACHERS SHARE THEMSELVES WITH OTHERS,
LEAVING BEHIND A BIT OF THEIR
ENERGY AND ENTHUSIASM..."

Before any of you were born, we built our small farmhouse in an old cornfield at the top of a narrow valley that runs from the Green Mountains due west toward New York State. As you know, most of our weather blows in from the west and in the summer when a storm moves in, I usher you all out to the narrow front porch so that we can watch storms sweep down Walnut Mountain or witness towering shrouds of mist, which change color and shape as they slowly drift up our dirt road. But when the weather comes from the east, we know it will be a hard blow. Last March, we had such a storm, a minitornado that ripped through our valley like a freight train, plucking out old maples and scattering the roofs of sheds and barns over the sodden, dormant fields.

After church on the Sunday following the storm, I picked up my chain saw and went over to help a neighbor cut up three large sugar maples that were now leaning precariously toward his house. I fired up my 16-inch Stihl and got started on the first tree, which had already been felled by the local woodsman, Harley, a born Vermonter.

As I cut down through the tree and got toward the bottom, the trunk started to close in and bind my saw. After a few minutes, I noticed that Harley was standing next to me with his own chain saw purring. He started cutting through the massive maple from the bottom up, and as he neared the top of the log, the cut would widen, leaving plenty of room for the chain. After a couple of cuts, he went away. I then realized he had just given me a silent lesson in chainsawing. He had quietly watched me do it the wrong way and in the great tradition of old-time Vermonters, Harley had stepped in and taught me a lesson without a word spoken between us.

Most of what I have learned about cooking has come not from experts telling me what to do but from watching others. In the early 1960s, I learned how to knead bread by watching Marie Briggs, our town baker, work the rich, nut-brown dough back and forth over a plastic red-checked tablecloth, her pale arms full of hidden muscle and sinew. On those rainy summer afternoons when I was helping out in the kitchen, not the hayfields, she treated me like an equal, expecting me to learn by watching. She quietly demonstrated how to stir up the fire in the woodstove that baked the bread, to cut out doughnuts, and to roll out sugar cookies. But thirty years later, I can't remember one word of explicit instruction. All those engaged in hard work were treated equally and accorded a large measure of respect. My terrible fear of disappointing Marie was her great strength as a teacher.

Since that day in March when Harley tutored me in chainsawing, I have spent many hours thinking about other teachers. I have shared the immense benefits of a hard day's work with Charles Bentley, a local farmer. I have witnessed the invigorating pleasures of giving help and assistance to others from Julia Child. I have seen the vivid joy of faith in the eyes of ushers at our church. I have been energized by the great intellectual curiosity of my mother. I have been softened and humbled by the total love and acceptance of each of you, which is bestowed upon occasion. I have learned to savor the idiosyncrasies of daily life from my father, a keen observer of the human condition. Good teachers share themselves with others, leaving behind a bit of their energy and enthusiasm even as we grow and move apart. What remains is the sharing, not so much the instruction itself.

The greatest teacher of them all gave His life so that we might learn from His sacrifice. Like a good Vermonter, He knew that action speaks louder than parable. He also knew that the act of teaching bestows rich rewards on the teacher as well as the student. So be eager to pick up the chain saw and whisk and venture out into the world, ready to be both a student and teacher, eyes open to lessons unspoken.

twenty-six

Vermont faces

"TAKE A MOMENT TO SEE YOURSELF
IN A MIRROR AND TAKE YOUR OWN MEASURE..."

———————————

O ver time, your face will tell a story, one that can be read by the thoughtful observer. It will be a story of how you have lived your life, whether you are partial to laughing out loud, or squinting into the bright sun that floods a hayfield, or perhaps standing apart, merely acting the role of witness. Here in the Green Mountains, the faces are broad and open, with a good stretch of cheek, smooth and flat like a choice piece of bottomland. The muscles underneath the smooth folds of skin are relaxed, not bunched and taut as in the faces of many city folk. This wide dinner plate of a face is usually set off with large, expressive ears, the lobes often distended, hanging freely from their sturdy frames. Unlike the narrow, pinched faces of those who live far from the land, the Vermont face is welcoming, like coffee hour at the Methodist church or the wide-open door at a potluck supper.

But I particularly love the eyes of a Vermonter. They are often deep set, the shelf of the brows offering good shade in summer and the crow's feet testifying to years of squinting, Vermonters not being partial to sunglasses. But once one gets by the thick folds of eyelid and the woolly line of bushy eyebrow, one is pulled up short by the hard, small orbs. They are flinty, but not cold. They impart warmth, but also a cool wait-and-see detachment, taking in everything with a hunter's stare, giving a newcomer the uncomfortable feeling that he is prey.

After a bit, one notices that Vermonters rarely blink. Their eyes do heavy work, unafraid to stare hard, to look for patterns of behavior, to get familiar with another, judging perhaps how they might react in a crisis or whether they would be capable of good, steady work if asked to help bring in a load of hay. Partnered with this flat, uncompromising glare of appraisal comes a sparkle of dry humor, a child's playful glance, one that is incongruous to flatlanders, a look that unsettles and can easily be mistaken for ill will. But it is this slight unbalance, this edge of wit, that provides the tension that makes a good Vermont face. It is the unexpected, the coiled sense of the absurdity of life that can strike out at any moment, catching one off guard. Look hard and you will see all of this in the eyes of a Vermonter.

In your faces I see much as well. Whitney, your face is carefully constructed and rigid, the features hard set in perfect proportion, like Venus carved from stone, perfectly preserved through the ages. You are a classic beauty, but with the piercing eyes of a judge, missing nothing and considering everything. It is your eyes that dominate, much like a Vermonter's, but perhaps with a touch less mirth and hard to read, even after all these years.

Caroline, it is your mouth that I watch most, full and sensual, most often in motion. You love the cadence of speech, the feel of sweet oatmeal on the palate, the pursing of the lips just before a kiss or nuzzle. You are a physical child, needy for warmth and understanding, for a hug and a kind word before bedtime. Your cheeks are full and your face long. You leave nothing unexposed except your deepest thoughts, which you keep carefully hidden, your childlike demeanor carefully crafted to lull the world into a false sense of confidence about who you are and what you want.

In Charlie's bright round face, I see the world. I see none of the complexity of your sisters, none of the swirl of hidden thoughts circling just beneath the surface. Every thought bubbles to the surface at once, your face incapable of hiding a grin or a great smile or even a burst of tears. You have a dedicated line from your brain to your face, a one-way high-speed transmission that provides instant communication. Your small perfect features often combine into a single burst of energy and emotion, the landscape changing instantly as each new thought passes by, usually discarded in mere seconds for more promising emotions. You are the enthusiast, the family cheerleader, the one who blunders forth undisturbed by subtleties or shades of meaning.

And finally, there is young Emily, just three months old as I write this. You have piercing eyes that are steadfast and true, eyes that remind me most of a Vermonter. At your young age, you already seem capable of independent thought and consideration. You smile when you want to, not when coaxed by others. Nothing is taken for granted. And you rock in your swing and watch the family parade by, recognizing, I like to think, your brother and sisters, trying to sort out the relationships and the family chemistry. Your face cannot tell me if you are to grow up soft and kind or with a harder, more self-involved edge, but no doubt you will be worthy of serious consideration, not a woman to be trifled with.

So as you make your way through life, look at the faces. Ignore the painted cheek and the perfect line of nose. Look deeper to see what the eyes can tell you about character. And most of all, take a moment to see yourself in a mirror and take your own measure. If you see the face of a Vermonter, be joyful. You will see much through your eyes, missing little of what life has to offer.

twenty-seven.

A glass half empty

"ALL THE RICHES
OF THE WORLD ARE WAITING FOR YOU..."

When I got home last night, Whitney, you anxiously directed me upstairs to my bedside table where a one-page typewritten note was waiting. You were once again feeling left out and unappreciated, the oldest of four, life never having been quite the same since your younger sister, Caroline, was brought into this world eight years ago. Now it is my turn to write you a note, to put down on paper how I feel about my firstborn, a young lady on the cusp of becoming a teenager, old enough to understand what I have to say.

Your blessing, Whitney, is a great intellect, a mind constantly considering facts as you see them, chewing over innocent slights and subtle shades of meaning to make sense of the world. This confidence in your raw brainpower makes you bold, quick to have an answer, and, I am afraid, too quick to draw conclusions. You are as beautiful as you are bright, a face molded with great distinction. Your almond eyes raise inscrutably skyward at their outer edges, their steely blue centers missing nothing. This unfiltered view of the world takes its toll. You bear the great burden of an adult's vision, seeing things that a ten-year-old ought not to confront so soon.

Behind this striking visage, your mother and I sense great turmoil and uncertainty. You know so much and yet you sometimes comprehend so little. I sense a gap between intellectual understanding and the ability to take in the emotional undercurrents that are part of family life. You need to know that you are loved unconditionally. You need to feel this deep inside of you, to carry this love with you to provide shelter and nourishment. Love and anger can share the same moment. A parent tired or disappointed with a child still acts out of love not hate, warmth not coldness, devotion not disappointment. To discover the power of unconditional love is what I wish most for you in life, so that you may give it to others and to recognize it when it is offered to you. Your mother and I give it to you freely. You were loved from the moment you were conceived and will be loved forever. I suppose that the love of a parent is much like God's love—though mortal, it is inspired out of something greater than ourselves.

But I suppose that your half-empty glass will not be filled soon. We are each molded out of different stuff, bits of old relatives strung together randomly to make a new being. You have been well blessed, Whitney, but cursed, too, with the pain of constant disappointment. Just try to remember the small moments as you grow up and put aside the broader currents. Take heart from the pancakes I make for your breakfast before school, the long bike rides down our country road, snowshoeing up the mountain in February, the morning sun brilliant on the thin, straight birches. Woven together, these little pieces of childhood will make whole cloth, a fabric that will hold together the rest of your life. Find in each of these moments the love others have offered you, that is there for the taking. They cannot be patched together with the mind but require an open heart to make them whole. As you grow into a woman, try to arrange the pieces to see the great pattern of your childhood, one of love and acceptance, not anger and frustration.

And finally, know that my heart is large enough to love your brother and sisters the way I love you; without reserve. The heart is infinite in its capacities—it expands like the universe, knowing no bounds. Nothing has been taken from you to give to them. They have simply added to your wealth, showing you the same love we do. It may not always be apparent. Love is not obvious, it requires a keen eye and an accepting heart.

All the riches of the world are waiting for you, for the moment when you put aside intellect in favor of heart, for what you know to be true deep inside your soul. It is not a moment that will come soon in your life, but it is what I wish most for you, for my oldest daughter who, for now, sees the glass half empty.

twenty-eight.

A day of contradictions

"You had your first taste of
bittersweet, disappointment and joy joining
together to offer you one of life's great secrets…"

When you turned eight, Whitney, I decided that
you should learn a bit about hard work, by helping
out a local farmer. Your first job was to help us corral a few
Belgians from the upper pasture above the old Lomberg farm
so they would be ready for our horse-drawn Fourth of July
parade. These were working animals, about sixteen hands high,
the size of a good quarter horse, and they didn't much like the
look of our rope halters. We funneled three of them into a
small spot by the gate, large maples on one side and a steep

bank on the other. But it was dangerous work. One of them spun up on his hind legs, muscled forequarters up and over the back of a second horse, taking flight through the woods.

It was no place for an eight-year-old, with the men shouting, the one-ton horses' ears back, nostrils flared, grain spilled on the muddy road. Sent far up the bank by an old sugar maple, you waited until we were done, left out, not needed. I looked up and saw the tears just starting down your cheeks. I had a sharp memory of times on the farm when I was young, rebuked for running a tractor downhill out of gear, pulling a fully loaded hay wagon, or standing helplessly by while the old-timers hooked up the teams to the old-fashioned mechanical mowers, snapping the ancient wooden hames around the collars, sorting out the tugs and traces, pole straps and lazy straps, whippletrees and eveners, britchens and back pads. It was a lonely time in those moments, unwanted and painfully aware that I was just a kid.

After the horses were safely in the barn, our family jumped into the pickup and went up to the Baptist hole just behind the old Methodist church. It's not really a hole, but a series of pools and chutes, used by generations of town kids and once used by ministers performing baptisms. It was late afternoon, the sun lighting up the crystal pools, turning the water a radiant green. I dove in, an icy baptism, came up to the surface and saw the dappled leaves, the rush of water, a hint of trout and moss-covered schist in the stream's moist, fresh scent, the sour taste of the heat of the day gone in an instant. And then all three kids followed, you jumping into my arms, exhilarated, happy, immersed in the rush of the stream and the wildness of the moment, suspended in time by the swirl of water, the sparkle of sun through the waving birches.

It was a day of contradictions, of disappointment and joy. But as it seemed later, the two events were intertwined, one needing the other. You had tasted first sour then sweet, the latter enhanced and made more joyous by the former. And on a day that ended with a yellow moon rising over the pale hollow, you had your first taste of bittersweet, disappointment and joy joining together to offer you one of life's great secrets.

twenty-nine.

Breakfast at the state line

"FREEDOM IS BOTH A LUXURY AND
A BURDEN, AN OPPORTUNITY TO CHOOSE
THE RIGHT PATH IN LIFE IF YOU HAVE THE COURAGE..."

W hen you were seven years old, Whitney, I used to take you out to breakfast at The State Line Diner. It's not much of an establishment, just a double-wide trailer set near the town line with a large Pepsi sign out front and old-fashioned sleigh bells on the front door. The plastic-sheathed menu was peppered with small ads for Day's Small Engine Repair, Downey's Rubbish Removal, Ushak's Supermarket, and Peabody & Bates Inc., the last offering screened and bankrun gravel. The waitress, in her best Vermont deadpan, always offered us "two minutes to decide what to order and one minute to eat it." The food is no more than one might expect, but the company was always good, from the farmers at the counter to the teenagers ordering up a mess of breakfast past noon.

I remember one Sunday in particular. After eggs sunny-side up, a few breakfast links, and a heap of toast, we hopped in my old orange Ford pickup and drove home by the back road. As we climbed slowly through the small mountain valley, I had a memory of you in the booth a few minutes before—quiet, beautiful, eyes wide open and self-assured. When you were younger, you lived in the moment, but now as you are starting to blossom, you have an eye to the future, no longer content to sit at a Formica tabletop, consumed by food and the attention of a parent. That day, you watched the great flow of people, aware of the possibilities, eager to take a few first steps on your own, away from the watchful eye of your father. The diner, like a railway car headed west, offered a new glimpse of the world and you had a vision of jumping on board as the train moved through this small, tired town, the wind scooping up your long blond hair, eyes squinting hopefully into the future.

As our truck came to a stop by the woodpile, I glanced across at you, noticing for the first time small changes in your face: a firmer chin, inquiring eyes, a hint of self-reliance and independence. These are the signs one looks for as a father, signals that a son or daughter has been raised well, trained to take his or her place in the world. The knot of affection between father and daughter is loosening a bit, and I am happy to give you more rope, more room to see the world on your own, to take those first tentative steps, to feel that rush of independence. It is your first intoxication, breathing in the full measure of freedom, seeing the great empty plains ahead of you without a guide or a map. These are giddy times, uncharted and full of sudden storms, but you have been born of sturdy stock, able to weather whatever lies in your path.

Just remember that freedom is both a luxury and a burden, an opportunity to choose the right path in life if you have the courage. Your path will be different than mine, so I can offer no map, just the knowledge that I am watching as you jump down from the cab and slowly walk away, your back turned to the old yellow farmhouse.

thirty.

See it through

"KEEP COMING BACK TO THE TASK AT HAND,
NO MATTER HOW IMPOSSIBLE IT MAY SEEM..."

———————

When I was ten, I got a summer job with a local dairy farmer, helping out with the afternoon milking as well as with haying, fixing equipment, and feeding and watering the horses. My first day started with an instruction to go out and bring in a cow with her newborn calf. The rest of the herd was already in the barn for the afternoon milking. I went out to the back pasture and soon found the wayward cow, horns long and untrimmed, standing protectively in front of her three-day-old. This wasn't the first time I had been around cows, but I was used to slow-moving, docile beasts. The kind I knew might step on your foot if you weren't careful, but they weren't mean or aggressive.

Knowing that I was being watched from the barn, I hitched up my pants and went right after her, confident that a slap on the rump and a few throaty "git-along" sounds would soon get the job done. When I was about thirty feet away, she lowered her massive horns and pawed the ground like a dyspeptic Texas longhorn. Then she came right after me. Luck was with me since the barbed wire fence was nearby, and I scrambled under it like a crab scuffling out of reach of a net, finding myself in a dense patch of milkweed and thistle. I looked up and saw her huge head, red eyes bulging out of massive bony sockets, a long ropy string of drool hanging from her lips.

For the next twenty minutes, I scooted out from the safety of the fence, made a series of wild herding movements with my arms, and then ran like crazy for safety. We finally worked our way around the perimeter of the pasture, the cow chasing me back to the great red barn. There the farmer, wearing a faded green cap and just the hint of a grin, came to my aid. He grabbed a thick leather milking strap, gave the cow a couple of good whacks, and she turned toward the barn, submissive and defeated. Somehow that farmer kept from laughing in the face of my utter humiliation, but that story is still told in our town, some thirty-five years later, since it so clearly defines what it means to be a Vermonter.

Yet for most folks these days, being a Vermonter has lost its meaning—like the lyrics to "Yankee Doodle Dandy," which no longer have the ring of familiarity. When one talks of persistence or thrift, these terms have little resonance in the modern vernacular. Confronted with a difficult, seemingly impossible task, an old-time Vermonter would simply settle in for the long haul. There was simply no alternative. New England farmers led a parsimonious life. If something broke, one had to repair it, since a new model was either not available or too expensive. And in the face of tragedy, Vermonters were always steadfast, never wavering in their conviction or inner sense of self-worth. One could do a lot worse than to live by the rules of the farm, no one person rising above the others, no pressing need to develop the inner self. Hidden desires are often best left hidden, our darker, more self-serving impulses sweated out in the hot July sun, our souls bleached white and pure through hard work.

So when your turn comes to go bring in the cow and the calf, don't flinch from the assignment. Run for cover if you must—I know I did—but stick to it. Keep coming back to the task at hand, no matter how impossible it may seem at the time. The old farmer watching you from the barn is looking for no more than persistence, the outcome being secondary to matters of character. Resist the temptation to turn tail and run for the barn. See it through and life will be your best friend, bestowing riches at every turn.

PART FIVE

Life on the Farm

thirty-one.

Hay day

"WE FILLED OUR MEMORIES WITH
THE JOY OF LABOR SHARED WITH OTHERS..."

———————————

Today is hay day, a bright, hot day, good for drying the long rows of timothy that have been cut with the binder and turned with a tedder in our neighbor's upper pasture. Standing by her barn, we watch the old red Massey Ferguson tractor draw the antique mechanical rake up and down the field, the hay turned into long furrows, ready for the baler. In the middle of the field, a wide swath of uncut hay stands as high as my chin. It is a thick harvest this year, the dense waves of grass brown and yellow near the ground then changing into a deep green in the middle of the stalks and then sliding into a paler hue toward the tops, the tight bundles of seed woven into a narrow sprouting.

I start the pickup and each of you hops on along with plenty of neighbors and their children. Everyone wants to help today, the blazing sun and light breeze a tonic for the long wet spring and dark cold winter. At first the bales slide onto the tailgate easily with a short jerk of the arms, but as we work our way toward the other end of the field, the flatbed starts to fill, bales packed in alternating directions, rising above the cab. It's time for the adults to heave to, throwing bales up onto the very top of the pile, giving them a final push as they roll onto the stack. The hay is dry and light this year, and the bales fly easily up into the air. It is this simple motion that I love most about haying. Planting the feet in front of a bale, grabbing the baling twine, lifting with a short jerk, bringing up the knee for an assist, the bale moving upward in a burst of antigravity. And then just at the top of its arc, the fingers release from the strings, palms are placed flat against the hay, and the whole body uncoils, sending the dry grass soaring up into the summer sky, high up onto the truck.

The hay is now loaded and we drive slowly down the road to the barn, bodies packed every which way into the cab or riding on top, hanging on in the rush of wind. I watch a light breeze as it catches the hay seeds on the hood of the truck, tiny doe-colored specs floating across a sea of brick red metal. I can feel the weight of the bales on the suspension, the truck traveling low and squat. We reach the rickety gray barn, and I back up the truck to the entrance. The children run through the dark opening, thin ribbons of light piercing the blackness, the smell of ripe hay and old manure comforting and singular. I climb on top of the stack and hurl bales down onto the barn floor, and each of you scurries about, dragging bales to the next man in line. I feel on top of the world, the rhythm of throwing the bales working into my system, the physical labor welcome and energizing. From my lofty nest, I can see the mountains sliding down into New York State, an old cornfield now overgrown with milkweed, and acres of hay ready to be cut and baled.

The last bale—the "one we've been looking for," as the farmers call it—has been heaved and we gather around the gallon milk jug that has been filled with springwater and mint and then frozen. Partially melted, the water is ice-cold and perfumed, the mint a pale, withered green now but still lively in the mouth. I pass the jug along to each of you and we share a moment on a hot July afternoon, simple field hands on a clear Vermont day. Working together, we filled the barn with hay for winter as we filled our memories with the joy of labor shared with others. And know that these are good memories, many hands busy with common purpose.

thirty-two

Tools of the trade

"WHEN YOU ARE DISCOURAGED, DIG
A HOLE IN THE EARTH AND THINK
OF THE POSSIBILITIES..."

Before you were born, the farmers in our small
Vermont town still mowed hay with a team of
horses, corn was harvested with a corn binder pulled by a
team of mules, and they even hayed small fields with a
pitchfork and wagon. Fields were planted with grain drills, a
wooden horse-drawn seeder with a row of metal cones that
made furrows in the soil for the seeds. The outhouse was in
use until 1969, most cooking was done on a wood
Kalamazoo stove, and wells were dug only after a dowser had

located the best spot, using a forked stick made from apple wood, the divining rod moving sharply downward in the presence of underground water.

I am only one generation removed from a time when every family farm was its own factory, churning out butter and cream, provisioning a root cellar, spinning wool, rendering lard, putting up preserves, making dandelion wine, boiling maple sap into syrup, collecting honey, and so on. In those days, farms were full of wood and metal machines, the labor-saving devices of the nineteenth century that carried over well into the twentieth. There were milk aerators and churns, yarn winders and corn graders, shredders and binders, root cutters and cheese presses, Felloe saws (used for cutting rounds of wood for wheels) and beetles (large mallets), hog hooks and marking gauges, barn scrapers, metal swing churns, cream separators, and the all-purpose Superior stainless milk pails. Ice was plowed and sawed, put onto sleds, and then moved by teams of horses to large ice houses where engine-powered conveyers lifted the heavy blocks high up to the upper levels. The blocks were then packed with sawdust, the ice house closed, and the heavy twenty-one-inch blocks would last well into summer.

Every August, we visit local fairs that often have museums or barns full of old equipment. I dutifully take you past the dog treadmills and the summer hearses (winter hearses had runners), the mailman's buggy with the built-in stove, the snow rollers (five-foot-high wooden rollers pulled by horses to pack down the snow), nickel-plated wooden stoves, phaetons and surreys, and displays showing old kitchens or children's bedrooms or the toolshed built onto the side of a barn. I eagerly enter the "What Is It?" contests or look hard at the old photos, hoping to see one of the old-timers I used to know or what the abandoned train station used to look like in 1910, when it was prosperous, an artery pumping the lifeblood of commerce into a small New England town.

I look into your eyes and see no connection, no interest in the process of turning milk into cream and butter or hay into feed or pigs into bacon. What used to be crucial to survival is no longer relevant. Perhaps gone with the fence tighteners and the ice tongs, we have also lost a bit of self-reliance and the association to how beginnings turn into endings. A well-made tool in knowledgeable hands is a wonderful thing; wood is cut and split, cream is churned into butter, a field is mowed in the afternoon sun, swallows swooping low looking for bugs that have lost their hidey-holes. Farmers are men of many trades, being planters and cultivators, veterinarians and blacksmiths, carpenters and mechanics, gardeners and weathermen. They could judge a horse or use an Eddy plough or dig a well. They could also teach their sons and daughters, passing along experience to the next generation. In that world, parents loomed large, for their experience and skill were readily apparent. A man who can grow corn to feed pigs or a woman who can put up food for the winter demonstrates his or her usefulness daily—and the kids are spectators to the accumulation and value of experience. Today, most parents have diminished roles, their expertise narrow and rarely seen, appreciated only by a small number of coworkers.

So in an age of specialists, take the time to be generalists. Piety is a good thing, but so is usefulness. Learn to fix what is broken. Take the time to master the shovel and the hoe, the hammer and the chisel. Plant a few apple trees and learn how to prune them. Know something about the soil, about compost and lime, about pH levels and organic matter, about how to control weeds and get rid of potato bugs. Learn your trees and your wild plants, picking a colander of fiddlehead ferns in the spring or a bunch of ramps or wild watercress when you see them.

Life is brimming with things to be discovered and known, skills to be mastered, challenges to be overcome. And when you are discouraged, dig a hole in the earth and think of the possibilities. So many things can be planted in your lifetime, skills that once mastered will bear fruit forever. Next year, walk those old barns with me and open your eyes wide with appreciation and reverence. Pluck up some enthusiasm for the business of life, for the loamy matter that supports us all. Become a handyman and spread your skills wide, digging deeper into the earth's crust to uncover its secrets.

thirty-three.

Little beekeepers

"THERE IS SOME UNDEFINED MAGIC BETWEEN
A FATHER AND HIS YOUNG SON..."

---

few years ago, your mother gave me an unusual
birthday present—a hive of Italian honeybees plus
a starter kit for the beginning beekeeper. This included a bee
suit, a helmet, gloves, and a smoker (a small metal canister
with attached bellows that, when filled with burning grass
clippings or burlap, produces smoke). Late one Friday night,
I picked up the twenty-five thousand bees in their hive,
placed them in the back of our van, and then deposited them
in a corner of our lower meadow. Since that day, I have added
another six hives and, by now, each of you have poured

gallons of the late-harvest thick, dark honey over just about everything you eat.

I'll never forget the day that the mail-order child-size beekeeping suit arrived. I had to go out and place Apistan strips in the hives; the honey supers had to be lifted off the top, the hive box had to be opened, and the strips, which are lethal to the mites, placed inside. Caroline, you spoke up quickly, wanting to be the first to put on the bright white cotton suit, so I zippered you into it. The headgear was attached to the body, and your round face blurred behind the fine mesh protective screen. You fussed with a long lock of sun-bleached blond hair that hung down in front of your nose. I had to help you unzip the hood so you could tuck it up behind your ear and out of the way.

As we walked out to the old Ford pickup, I noticed that your three-year-old brother, Charlie, was tagging along, but he seemed unusually quiet. I stooped down and looked into his saucer face under the sharp line of blond bangs and saw that he was crying, tears slipping quietly down his fat cheeks. He wanted to wear the suit and help his dad with the bees. I explained that the suit was too big for him and that he would have to grow up a bit before he could wear it. That only made things worse, but I helped him up into the cab anyway, loaded up my gear, and we set off down into the lower meadow.

We had work to do with a couple of other hives first and, Caroline, you stood right next to me, brave and attentive, as I lifted off supers, checked the queens, and made some adjustments with the frames that hold the honeycomb. It was a fine July morning, a light breeze flowed in from the west. The bees were docile, a few scouts buzzing around our heads but lacking conviction and spunk. I stood up for a minute to stretch and looked over to see Charlie in the cab, his sad small face peering through the rear window, tear-stained and deflated. Poor Charlie was quite a sight, all the fight having drained out of him, some primal connection with his dad having been broken, like leaving your best rabbit dog at home on the first day of the season. So there was nothing else to do. I went up the window and told him it was his turn.

Well, it was as if Santa Claus had walked out of a stand of nearby poplars. He had been brought back from exile, his face once again animated, the silence broken by an earnest interest in the suit itself and how it would go on, like an astronaut called to duty at the last minute. But to say that the suit was too big was no exaggeration. On Charlie, the sleeves drooped down a good foot past the hands, the headgear huge and inflated, looking like a low-budget sci-fi movie. But we made do, stuffing the extra two feet of leggings into his rubber workboots and pushing his hands into the huge gloves, the fingers flopping empty and flat.

There is some undefined magic between father and son at such a young age. Each of us has something useful to offer the other, the father conferring the prestige of entering into adulthood through shared responsibility and the son bringing new life to old routines through unbridled zeal and enthusiasm. The father, at first secure in his role as teacher, soon finds himself on a slippery slope; the child, through innocence and the ability to live in the moment, offering something of greater value. Charlie and I stooped low over the hives as two shadows stretched boldly across frames full of thick clover honey. One was large and still and the other was small but lengthening in the morning sun, his large white beekeeping suit filled with pride and determination.

thirty-four.

Looking back

"IT'S GOOD TO GLANCE BACK NOW AND THEN,
JUST TO CHECK WHERE WE HAVE COME FROM..."

---

arm work often entails looking back to see where you have come from. I look back over the tractor to see if the bush hog has missed any grass on the last turn or to make sure that it is set at the proper height as I mow down a steep hill. I look back at the planter in spring to make sure that the seed is planted deeply enough or to check if the rototiller needs another pass through the row. One always looks back to other growing seasons when the honey was darker or the apple blossoms thicker or perhaps the weather drier. And as I grow older, I look back to times when fields were mowed with a team, the chatter of the sickle bar and clicking of the gears common currency back then, but now are rare coinage, the teams brought out only on special occasions.

The other day, Caroline, you and I were walking down to pick some corn across the road, and I looked back and saw something unexpected. Your skin was stretched over the form of a young woman who was slowly fitting the outer membrane to her bulkier frame. Your face had become longer and a bit wiser, your childish grin taking on a more serious undertone, as if you had something sadder and more complicated to communicate. I looked back and remembered my fatted cherub when you were just three, standing on Nantucket, framed by a spray of TK roses on weathered fence, face bursting with a smile and the simplicity of childhood as the shutter clicked. I look back and remember the two of us holding hands, your instructions quite specific about the proper amount of pressure to exert—enough to communicate the tight bond between father and daughter but not enough to cause discomfort. I look back and see tears of disappointment, a face streaked with rivulets of humiliation caused by the insecurity of an older sister. I look back and feel the warmth of a nuzzle, your good cheer and bright countenance in need of constant fill-ups through close proximity to those who love you.

But most of all, I look back and see snapshots of you growing up on that narrow dirt road than runs by our house. In the evenings after dinner, we often take a walk to visit neighbors or watch the sunset. At first, you were carried, your tiny face peeking out of a blue bandanna wrapped loosely to keep out the cool evening air. And then you walked between your mother and I, arms stretching upward, swung up into the sky, red sneakers launched into an arc of child's play and whirlwind motion. And then you went piggyback, your short legs no match for the evening constitutional, your tiny fat hands locked together under my chin or across my face. And then you made your own way, legs pumping up and down like pistons gone awry, balance maintained only through the divine grace that looks after small children. Finally, you were on your own, a new baby brother taking your place in his mother's arms.

One evening, as we made our way down to the small red barn by the chicken coop, you begged to be swung like a windmill through the twilight. In that moment, you were looking back to another time and saw yourself as a younger child. Like good farmers, both of us know how to sit high on a tractor that is moving forward and still glance back now and then, just to check where we have come from so that we know where we are going.

thirty-five.

The mug-bread
turns out fine

"I WAS PROUD, BUT ALSO FILLED WITH
THE JOY OF THE UNEXPECTED..."

When all of you were younger, I used to read you stories from *Old Squire's Farm*, written by C. A. Stephens, who describes his life growing up on a large Maine farm with plenty of brothers, sisters, and cousins all under the same roof. One of my favorite stories—since it involves food—concerned his grandmother's mug-bread, so named because it was started in a lavender-and-gold-banded white porcelain mug. In the evening, she would mix "two tablespoons of cornmeal, ten of boiled milk, and half a teaspoonful of salt in that mug, and set it on the low mantel shelf behind the kitchen stove funnel, where it would keep uniformly warm overnight." At breakfast time, his grandmother would peer into the mug to see if the little "eyes" had begun to open in the mixture. If everything worked out as planned, water and flour were stirred in and the mixture was put back on the shelf to rise until lunchtime. It was baked into "cartwheels"—foot-wide, yellow-brown loafs just an inch thick that were served with fresh Jersey butter and all the canned berries a boy could eat. But some mornings, the mug would disappear suddenly and a strong sulfurous smell would linger in the kitchen. In that case, the wrong microbe had "obtained possession of the mug." One never knew how it was going to turn out. It was this element of chance, the not knowing, that made that mug-bread taste so fine.

Every town has a coming-of-age ritual, a rite of passage that often has unexpected outcomes. Over these many years, I have taken each of you in turn up to the cave in Beartown at the mouth of the Green River. On the day when each of you has been ready to negotiate the long, dark passage, I have mounted an expedition.

The first outing was back in 1995, when you, Whitney, had just turned seven. You have always been a bit shy and never the first to rush into the unknown, so I was apprehensive about the trip. With some friends, we packed a bunch of local kids onto the flatbed of our old Ford pickup, equipped with candles, matches, big rubber boots, and a bag of cookies to celebrate our success. The truck was left at the end of the road, and we walked up through an abandoned camp, then to the mouth of the cave, where each child was given a candle. I went first, with five kids in line behind me, and you were in the middle of the pack.

The cave entrance is narrow and small—about five feet high—and the stream than runs through it is deep and cold. In the weak half-light of the candles, we crabbed back to a large circular room where we climbed up a funnel to the next level. The cave narrowed considerably at this point, and I made my way to the end where water bubbled up from a deep spring. I looked back and saw your mud-streaked face in the flickering glow. You looked confident and gave me a quick, intimate smile that said, "I did it." The other kids were far behind in the darkness, too scared to follow. You called out, "Come on, what are you guys afraid of?" I was proud, of course, but also filled with the joy of the unexpected. It was the journey together that provided the yeast that day, struggling through the dark cave, not knowing if you would make it all the way to the end. Next year it would be your younger sister Caroline's turn, but that could wait. On that hot August day, the mug-bread had turned out just fine.

thirty-six.

Side by side

"WE ARE ALL SEEKERS
OF SIGNS, WHICH ARE OFFERED TO
TRAVELERS WHO SIT SIDE BY SIDE IN SILENCE..."

It was a hot summer day when you, Charlie, and I took our first trip together in the pickup, down to the feed store in the next town. I buckled you in, your short legs reaching just over the front edge of the seat, your brown and yellow boots dangling in midair. The cab of the pickup was an open toolbox—screwdrivers, wrenches, fishing gear, and a hammer strewn about the seat and floor. You were eager to get on the road, chatting excitedly, head swiveling from right to left so as not to miss the smallest detail of the journey.

The old red Ford F150 wound down through the notch in the mountains and made its way to lower ground, where the air was hot and still. We were traveling south, the pickup following the exhaust strip painted down the middle of our lane. We passed an old dairy farm with a blue-and-white sign advertising registered Jersey cows as the rusted muffler percolated with a throaty growl. The sputtering launched out into the air and then entered the cab through your open window. The heat and the wind and the deep rumble of pistons and gears became sudden company, washing away conversation. We listened to the voice of the machine: the humming sound of rubber on pavement, the hollow jostle of the tailgate, the rhythmic back and forth, up and down of the crankshaft.

I looked over at you and found that you were staring my way, mouth slightly parted, eyes open but unaware. Then you curled up, changed position, hands gripping the window frame, your small fingers perched tentatively on the brown vinyl. The wind riffled your coarse, short blond hair. You tucked your legs under you, watching the mountains and hollows slide by in a daydream; hot, dusty, unmoving.

And I looked into your face as you drifted off to sleep and saw signs left by the creator—the blossoming of the divine seed that is planted in all of us. We are all seekers of signs, of clues to other kingdoms, which are offered to travelers who sit side by side in silence, fathers and sons together on life's journey. Like old farmers, we watch for a tilt of the head, an unexpected pause or a sidelong glance and see a window into a greater universe. Old men sit in pickups, on old sofas, and on sagging front porches in silence, dreaming of worlds glimpsed darkly and days gone by when their sons sat next to them as they drove down hot, dusty roads.

thirty-seven.

A ragtag family

> "IT WAS THE JOURNEY,
> NOT THE DESTINATION, THAT COUNTED..."

On a bright Saturday afternoon last summer, the whole family took a long hike—through the hollow behind our farmhouse, up logging roads, across dry creek beds, and up to a small clearing that looks down over the hills of New York State, a sea of leafy mounds dense with foliage and unbroken by signs of civilization. We provisioned well: meatloaf sandwiches, ripe plums, a bit of cheese, water and juice boxes, blueberries, and a small cache of candy (a lure for any laggard child). Knapsacks were shouldered, four-month-old Emily was strapped into her Snugli, work boots were laced up tight, and we brought our field guides with us to identify trees, salamanders, newts, scat, and tracks in the mud.

We strode by our hayfields, short and green after the first cutting, and then entered the woods where a large patch of blackberries grows. It was mid-August and there were plenty of berries left, so we stopped to pick them. We left the small hard berries untouched, reaching instead for ripe, juicy specimens that burst in the mouth. Whitney, you and I did most of the picking, while Charlie and Caroline stood their ground and waited to be fed, like young chicks in a nest. Minutes passed, although we weren't counting, and then we started up again, heading now toward the landing at the bottom of the hollow, the spot where in years gone by, loggers piled the shorn trunks, skidded through the undergrowth, pulled by chains and a large diesel motor. The clearing has healed now, carpeted with a good growth of weeds and goldenrod, a few old trunks half rotted off to the side.

We crossed the streambed that runs down the hollow and then followed the logging road that parallels it up the mountain. A few yards ahead, the stream still carried a small trickle of water, the thin waterfall now a drip, the pool below a puddle. We searched for fish and salamanders, following the stream for a hundred yards or so and then coming back to the old road. We then made our way past the spring, the one that runs out of a small copse of fern down onto the road, turning the track to mud and gravel, much of the topsoil having been washed off. Charlie, you blundered through, looking for the wettest spot, the one that would provide the best squish and squelch as you landed soundly on the heels of your feet.

We found a spring peeper or wood frog, about the size of a quarter, hopping across the road. We picked it up and carried it a while, caged in cupped hands, handed back and forth among you kids. We discovered immature acorns on the ground and picked leaves, easily identifying red from sugar maples but having more trouble with the elms and oaks, the latter having somewhat thinner leaves but otherwise quite similar to elms. We looked high up into the upper canopy searching for a hawk's nest. We could hear its stationary cry, piercing and wild, surprisingly profound in timbre, full of meaning, we guessed, for whatever was listening. We picked up walking sticks and investigated nicely shaped pieces of quartz with creamy white veins. We took a rest where the road split, deciding which way to turn.

An hour had gone by and we were only a bit closer to our destination. It seemed that we weren't actually headed in a straight line, the six of us more interested in the road we were traveling than where we might end up. We were a ragtag family that day, lacking in dedicated purpose, walking down side roads, delighting in detours, heads bent to the ground—not chin up, gazing into the future. And then we were past the logging road and into the woods, headed up the top of the gully where there is a natural pasture, wooded but with small patches of clearings, where the sunlight bursts unfiltered onto the bright green saplings hopeful of achieving greatness in the years to come. And in this spectral glade, we moved slowly under large fallen trunks, over small deadwood, and around thick stands of birch and large boulders. All of a sudden, we had arrived at our picnic spot, a large fall of mature oak that offered good seating.

As I handed out sandwiches and fruit, I thought that it was the journey that day, not the destination, that counted. In the woods, time is often suspended, the trail made easier through observation. We had taken note of the leaves and the bark, the tracks of deer and bear, of a hawk circling high above the trees, of the stones and saplings, of the trickle of water in the brook, and the taste of blackberries warmed by the sun. We had simply paid close attention that day and had been rewarded with a journey that was itself the destination. A simple lesson perhaps, but one that is easily forgotten.

thirty-eight.

Walking in my footsteps

"EVEN WHEN YOU
HAVE FOUND OTHER HEROES,
I WILL STILL WANT TO BE JUST LIKE YOU..."

Just last summer, Charlie, I ordered you a toy shotgun, a double-barreled model with miniature shells that can be loaded up with small disposable charges. Once you knew it was coming, you asked me every few minutes if it had arrived, your eyes popping, your voice stopping and starting with nervous excitement. When the box finally did show up, you became perfectly still, like a religious pilgrim trying to grasp the sheer magnificence of the Sistine Chapel in one thirsty, reverent look. From that moment on, the gun has hardly left your side, slung over your shoulder or waved about, the long barrel unwieldy in your short arms.

You soon decided that we were to go coyote hunting—no doubt because these creatures' wild cries are a common sound at night as they race through our valley, up around the house, the noise piercing your sleep, waking you to a world as strange as your dreams. I loaded up my twelve gauge and you put on your leather cartridge belt, loaded with brightly colored shells, and we set out into the woods. I watched you as you watched me, trying to hold your gun just like me, the safety catch on, the barrel pointed toward the ground. As I shifted its position, changing hands, you did the same, a small mirror held up to my actions, a short bundle of enthusiasm and energy walking in my shadow.

The house was soon left behind, its roof no longer visible, and we were on our own, walking in single file. As soon as the trees started to close in on the sides of the logging road, you wanted to know where the coyotes were, expecting their large gray shapes to suddenly appear, offering themselves broadside, so that we might take a shot. Then you started to ask about bears and lions, wondering if they might suddenly shoot out of the undergrowth, startling us like Dorothy on her way to Oz. And then it struck me that you were walking through your dreams, wild things just out of sight, the woods alive with half-imagined shapes—minotaurs and satyrs, lions and bears, and enormous black wolves that might swoop down off the hillside and carry you away. Your gun was held tightly now, your step right next to mine, conversation temporarily hushed as we walked deeper into the woods.

And then, a funny thing happened. I started to scan the woods for large game, half expecting to see a black bear or a pack of coyotes loping along a ridge. I was in your world now, part of your imagination, the woods seen through the eyes of a three-year-old.

Later, as we walked back out into the sunshine, the roof of the farmhouse just visible behind the side hill, you were still walking just like me, holding your shotgun as I had showed you. I started to think that fathers and sons trade back and forth, dads offering rather pedestrian knowledge of the world in return for the wonders of the universe, glimpses of places we haven't been since childhood, short bursts of color and imagination that burn brightly but quickly. For a few years yet, you will want to be just like me, carrying a real gun, not a toy, tall, experiencing the world like a man. But in time, that will pass. And even when you have found other heroes, I will still want to be just like you, on a sunny day in May, when we walked through the woods, and you showed me so much that I had forgotten.

PART SIX

Times of Celebration
and Remembrance

thirty-nine.

A guide for the
Christmas season

"HAPPINESS IS IN INVERSE PROPORTION
TO THE NUMBER OF THINGS ONE OWNS..."

I recently met a fishing guide up on the Matapedia River in Canada. Richard, who was born in 1910, is a bowman for the Cold Spring Camp, springing into action once one of the "sports" hooks a salmon, the biggest running up to forty pounds or more. The fish must be allowed to run, the drag on the reel has to be set properly, and the large three-man canoe must be poled into the proper position to land the fish. Over half the big ones are lost before they can be reeled in due to improperly tied flies (smart fish bang their heads against a rock to dislodge the hook) or lines that get tangled in debris or the canoe itself. For a man of eighty-eight years, Richard moves quickly, like a large cat that dozes most of the day but has stores of coiled energy waiting to be released.

One afternoon, I stopped by his double-wide trailer to visit. He told me that when he was growing up, everyone had a large family, and Richard's was no exception. There were eight children, four of whom are still alive. His mother tended a garden of turnips, potatoes, carrots, cabbage, beets, and beans, and she kept much of it in a root cellar over the winter. Cream was stored in metal cans in the brook throughout the summer, or hung by broom handles into barrels of cool water. Ice was cut in the winter and stored with sawdust or hay as insulation in the ice house. His mother used to make brown sugar fudge, molasses cookies, raisin pie, marble cake, dried apple pie, cucumber and mustard pickles, pumpkin jam, and doughnuts. Most every family used to raise a few pigs and some beef. For Thanksgiving, the family would have a roast chicken and a glass of wine. For Christmas, he would get a stocking filled with a few apples, an orange, and some hard candy.

Richard left school at age fourteen, running off to the logging camps where he would spend most of his life. The first of October, they would start cutting either up from the river or off one of the tributaries using two-man saws. By Christmas, the cutting would stop and the logs would be hauled by horse down to the rivers, where they were floated downstream. Logjams were common, a crew of eighty men used to do about five miles a day on the river, the logs getting stuck in a "wing jam" or on a rock. The camp cooks served baking powder biscuits, beans, and plenty of black tea for breakfast. There were no chickens or eggs—the only chicken Richard ever saw on those drives was "the one in the picture on the wall."

With white, bushy sideburns and dressed in thick woolen pants, Richard sat on the narrow porch attached to the trailer. With legs outstretched, he recalls with relish the plate of beans and biscuits for breakfast, the long workdays hauling logs with the teams, the sweet smoke from hot campfires, and the winter days spent rabbit hunting. He used to sell rabbits for twenty-five cents apiece to the hotel down in Sillarsville.

Listening to Richard revel in his memories of hard work and simple pleasures, I'm reminded again that happiness is in inverse proportion to the number of things one owns. The clothes on one's back, a warm, dry place for the winter, a good job, a few friends, and a bit of loose change make a happy man. Happiness is being needed—not needing things.

So during this fall season, our family tries to take pleasure in routine chores, making coffee cake for church or greasing and storing equipment for the winter. We read up on beekeeping and pruning and the best methods for ridding ourselves of next year's crop of potato beetles. We spend time watching the view from our farmhouse, the light thinner now and the air so clear that we can look out across our valley and make out individual leaves, five-pointed sugar maples, shagbark hickory, or the long, slender leaves of white ash.

As we sit on our front porch, we wonder about the upcoming holidays. Perhaps this is the year we will make do with a roast chicken, a glass of wine, a raisin pie, and a stocking filled with tangerines and hard candy for each of you. In this day and age, it is a wistful thought, an idea to be hoped for, a fantasy just on the fragile edge of possibility. But in a season that was born of simplicity and faith in God, we could all learn from Richard and find salvation in a plate of beans, a biscuit, and a cup of strong tea. I like to think that happiness and grace would follow us the rest of our days.

forty.

Little Easter eggs

"Everyone has a secret life in which
the aged are children and the weak are strong..."

One of our family's long-standing traditions is to visit your grandmother's house on Easter weekend, the highlight of which is the egg hunt Sunday morning. For each of you, the rules are simple. The eggs are placed out in the yard, near the chicken coop, up in the rafters of the barn, hidden in the beds of pachysandra and daffodils, tucked up in the corner of a bird feeder, or slipped between stacked logs in the woodpile. The hunt starts late morning, after we return from church, each of you clutching a large rough basket in the mudroom, jostling to be the first out the door. Small faces peek out of the windows, looking for a flash of yellow or blue, marking early destinations. Then the door is opened and the race is on.

The Berkshires are usually cool on Easter morning, the sky a backdrop of light blue streaked with silvery clouds, which pass over the barnyard like ships, swallowing us in their shadow. The air is transcendent and clear, each blade of grass and spilled grain of birdseed is perfectly silhouetted against the bare ground. I watch you hunt furiously, Charlie, hand in hand with your grandmother, her step slow and a bit unsteady as you pull her forward, always on the verge of tumbling into disaster, a pile of legs and arms gone awry. For each of you, the hunt is pure action, a pile of wildly colored eggs to be found and gathered into a basket, then counted to determine who was this year's winner.

But for your grandmother, the hunt is more complicated. She is seeking something more elusive, to pick up each of you like bright eggs and cradle you tenderly, letting flow the great reservoir of love that she has stored over these years. She is a miser, a spendthrift with her affections, unwilling to risk tender moments. Yet in her eyes one can see the pressure of this vast lake, the water coming easily with a simple hug or kiss or during an awkward moment of parting. You are her chicks and she is the mother hen, steadfast and parsimonious, a stern parent set in her ways. I like to think that she yearns to run once again through the cool breeze of April, grabbing at the yellow, green, and blue eggs, throwing them helter-skelter into her basket, laughing and letting go. But she stands instead and watches, enjoying a quiet sip from the great river of activity that is running before her.

After she is gone, I ask that you remember not the lone figure standing on the edge of your childhood, rarely seen or heard, but instead dream of her beside you on those Easter mornings, shouting, running, pushing you aside to find the next egg. On those days she was a child again in spirit, side by side with each of you, holding hands, exuberant, full of life and energy. Remember that, like your grandmother, everyone has a secret life in which the aged are children and the weak are strong. Don't judge a book by its cover, but take a moment to read a few pages before setting it aside. There are great riches to be found in strangers if you only take the time to look for them.

forty-one.

Everyone loves a parade

"THE ROOTSTOCK OF THIS TOWN
GROWS STRONG IN ITS MODEST EXPECTATIONS..."

O ne of the great events in our small Vermont town, the
one each of you enjoy the most, is the July 4th parade.
It's a hodgepodge of horse-drawn wagons, tractors, buggies,
breaking carts, and even a team of oxen, proceeding single file
up from the yellow farmhouse to the Methodist church. I don't
know how many more years we'll continue this tradition, so
before it goes the way of the divining rod and wood cookstove,
I thought I would commit it to paper.

We arrive midmorning and I head over to the lower barn
to help harness the workhorses in their stalls, the wood slats

rough-sawn and hung with bridles and rope halters. Left wild up in high pastures during the summer, these are one-ton workhorses whose flanks reach to my chin, their massive, shod feet skittish on the wooden floorboards, unused to confinement and the scent of men. Junior Bentley, the town's last farmer, keeps up a steady conversation punctuated by sharp rebukes, asking the horses if they know what they are doing, his voice deep but rising quickly when the need arises, trying to bring order to a mass of buckles and straps draped over the dusty, short-haired flanks of these wary, stiff-eared beasts. We buckle on the collars, slinging the harnesses over, settling on the hames, hooking it into place, and then pull the britchens over the rumps. When I was a kid working in this old barn, the workhorses had men's names such as Duke or Dan. Now that times have changed, I help harness up Snowdrop or Tiffany or Queen, hardly what one would expect from an animal that weighs as much as a pickup.

Each of the men brings one of the horses out of the barn and then we hitch up the teams to the wagons. The pole straps usually need adjusting and the team has to be backed up into the whippletrees and hooked up in the right sequence. This is where experience counts. One wrong move and the horses can easily become tangled up or spooked. Meanwhile, milling about in front of the yellow farmhouse is an odd mix of locals and weekenders. One local woman, Georgie, is usually dressed as Uncle Sam, Susie De Peyster wears a black stovepipe hat, and a few old-timers sit quietly in their buggies, round and unleavened from a diet of pot roast and biscuits. Once the big teams are hitched, however, there is no time to lose as the large workhorses are restless and anxious to move.

Every year, I play banjo in the band, our repertoire limited to "Grand Old Flag," "The Caisson Song," "America the Beautiful," "Yankee Doodle Dandy," and "American Patrol," which features a solo on the recorder. We also have a banged-up tuba, a flute, a clarinet (played by the minister), a keyboard, sometimes a fiddle, and one drum. Small groups of neighbors stand by the road or sit in old collapsible chairs, their webbing frayed from the sun and years of use. The wagon sways back and forth, the horses' hooves clip and clop on the pavement, and their tails swish back and forth. In the old days, of course, everything was pulled by horse up and down this main road: sawed chair seats, brushbacks and barrels from the half-dozen small factories, supplies headed up to Minor Heard's general store, and sawed lumber coming down from the mill and headed over to Cambridge or points south. This means of transportation has much to recommend it, offering time for good conversation as we gossip about the neighbors or the state of the second cutting.

After the parade, we meet for a cookout at the corner house with well-done hamburgers cooked on an ancient gas grill, pasta salads, baked beans, a huge metal can full of sweet iced tea, a sheet cake frosted in the design of the American flag. And, of course, there are plenty of kids with freckles and mischief in their open, country faces. Last year, one of them was caught dragging the flag on the ground and got a good talking to by an old-timer who was wearing his U.S. Navy cap. These things are taken seriously in Vermont.

Our town is a like a large congregation, made up of many generations from grandmothers to great-grandchildren, dependent on the quiet pleasures of routine and modest expectation. There is little regard for the new in this high mountain valley, where dependability takes the measure of a man. Someday you, Charlie, may take my place hitching the horses to the whippletrees, or perhaps you, Caroline, will play the banjo or flute in the parade where I used to sit on that rickety flatbed that held the band members. On every July 4th from now until the river stops flowing, the sound of Grand Ol' Flag will resonate off the mountains and the parade will work its way up to the old Methodist church. The rootstock of this town grows strong in its modest expectations and delight in the familiar, soil that nourishes our children during the brief summers of their childhood.

forty-two.

Harvest days

"DARKNESS IN THE COUNTRY
BREEDS IMAGINATION..."

———————————

Each summer, your mother and I take you over to New York State, where we enjoy a Harvest Day celebration. We browse the collection of old balers, threshers, chain saws, corn huskers, tractors, bulldozers, tedders, Model Ts, wagons, silage machines, horse-drawn corn binders, and plenty of one-cylinder gas-powered engines. There are demonstrations of spinning wool plus plenty of picnic tables where one can buy homemade potato chips and a good pancake breakfast or hamburgers and the like for lunch. Soda is kept in an old white refrigerator by the barn. All food is bought and paid for on the honor system, the cashier friendly but with an undercurrent of authority, just enough to keep everyone honest.

My favorite exhibit is a rotting country store with a Tydol Gas Pump manufactured by Gilbert and Barker. Nailed to the front porch are old signs, including one for Larking and Knulson, "Furniture and Undertaking," perhaps an unlikely pairing unless one considers coffins furniture. Another sign suggests that one "Eat at the Green Parrot Café." The sign from the old covered bridge is hung just above the baked goods tent, admonishing folks not to drive faster than a walk over the bridge or suffer a five-dollar fine.

On our farm, we have our own harvest days, when the silver queen corn is ripe, the corn silk dark brown, and the ears are thick about the waist with large, ripe, golden silver kernels, plump and filled with sweet juices. Just when the corn has reached perfect maturity, bugs attack the ends of the ears, crows swoop down between the long rows, and raccoons start to knock over stalks, taking just a few bites from each ear.

I remember one night in particular last summer. It was a Sunday evening, the valley suspended in twilight, and I took the three of you older children down to the cornfield to pick corn and dig potatoes for a late supper. We took the old lantern, a shovel, and two paper bags, and the four of us marched across the dirt road, Charlie on my hip, excited by this small adventure. Soon we were walking through the rows, a wealth of lantern light spilling over broken, yellow stalks and half-eaten ears, leafy shadows spinning over the nearby pumpkin patch.

As the darkness dropped softly upon us, cloaking our small band of adventurers, we were swept up out of time into the pages of *Treasure Island*, the smell of cheap rum and the sound of the one-legged man upon the steps of the Admiral Bembo Inn clear as could be in the warm night air. Or perhaps we were running the Mississippi with Huck and Jim, eyes peeled for a campfire or the sound of other drifting voyagers bringing with them the scent of danger. The feel of the rough, ribbed husks and the warmth of the dry soil as we dug for potatoes were real enough, but darkness in the country breeds imagination. The skittish rustle of a chipmunk can easily be mistaken for a pigtail pirate, or the smell of fern and wet grass from the banks of our small stream can transport you to a Mississippi backwater. Night had dipped its outstretched wing and taken us aboard, up and away from the brightly lit order of daylight to a witching hour of a child's making. We soared from one current of imagination to the next, plunging into a vortex of fear and astonishment at the hoot of a bear and then up again into the cool night sky at the thought of buried treasures.

And, for my part, I was here in a small cornfield on a summer's night, no longer a father but just a child, alive with night's great possibilities, surrounded by my three treasures, leading me on through the darkness, illuminated by the spill of lantern light and a child's giddy imagination.

forty-three.

We'll visit when we're gone

"WILL OUR TIME TOGETHER GROW
AND PROSPER WITH AGE LIKE
A STURDY SUGAR MAPLE..."

———————

Standing in the remains of a small stone foundation, I see the ghosts. I smell the sizzle of venison steak and taste a pull of moonshine from the jug, as if the spectral hunters were still in camp. The church on a bright Sunday morning still carries for me the image of old Charles Bentley Sr., laid out in his best farmer's suit, in his open coffin, peaceful but already gone to the other side. When I drive by the spot where our old barn used to stand, I see the hand-forged sign for Green River Farm. I hear Bernie Squires, the caretaker and logger, his great barrel chest wheezing painfully from emphysema, barely able to catch and hold a breath.

During band practice for the Fourth of July parade held in the corner house, I see a row of old bachelors, their heavy pants held up by braces, sitting stoutly on the faded green sofa, more than one cane leaning up against the wall. A visit to the waterfall across the road from our old log cabin frees memories of cool summer mornings, the thunder of the water apparent long before I could see the spout of icy mountain brook shoot down into a deep bowl of water, sunlight piercing the heavy stand of pines. And the rhythmic thumping of a hay baler, even when just a whisper, floating up the valley, is enough to bring me back to a hot July afternoon, sweat stinging my eyes, the chaff from the dry hay in my mouth and ears and down my shirt.

As I get older, I wonder what each of you may carry in your memories when your mother and I are gone. When you stand still in a cornfield in the moonlight, will you hear me whispering to you in the rustling of the stalks? When you first hear the sound of a tractor starting up, will you think, just for a second, that I am still with you, going out to till the potato field? Will a taste of dark honey transport you to a field in twilight, standing with your mother and I, watching the bees float down into the hive, heavily laden with sweet nectar? Will the first fresh taste of ice cream on a hot day recall walking down our dirt road after dinner, a thousand lightning bugs sparking over a thick field of timothy and rye, ambling toward home where we spoon down great bowls of apple crisp and blueberry cobbler? Will a suddenly familiar look or glance pierce the thin veil between now and then, collapsing the intervening years since you are still a child held tight in my arms or sitting proudly in the cab of the pickup?

Or are memories weaker spirits, unable to conjure up the past except in faded whispers? Will our time together grow and prosper with age like a sturdy sugar maple or will the past mature early and wither? Can your mother and I fill you with good memories, stock each of you like root cellars for the long winter that comes after the abundant joy of childhood? It is only a guess, but I suspect that memories are fickle, choosing themselves instead of being selected by others. We cannot guess what will remain of the years spent at this yellow farmhouse after we are gone. It might be the little things—the way the lace curtains fill with breeze or the buzz of hummingbirds darting back and forth to the porch feeders. But if you listen hard, you will hear your mother and I in the driving rain against the side of the farmhouse or the murmur of the brook, memories that call out your name with hope and good wishes for the future.

forty-four.

Ghosts in the twilight

"FOR OUR FAMILY,
THE PAST IS STILL THE PRESENT..."

Late every August, we used to drive over to the Washington County Fair, where you flocked to the bumper cars, the flying school bus, the spinning tea cups, and the haunted double-wide trailer. For my part, I looked forward to a quiet stroll through the barns, admiring the Ayshires, Jerseys, and Holsteins with names like Becca, Winnie, Orea, and Brittany. Teenage girls tend to them in the night, forking away the fresh manure and straw, using electric razors to trim unsightly whiskers that might lose them points during the judging. In the 4-H tent, there always was an exhibit of garden produce, including beets, onions, carrots, peppers, tomatoes, and sweet corn, as well as vegetable art featuring cabbage faces and squash monsters. Local trees were also featured, with leaves from slippery elm, basswood, sassafras, white Ash, shagbark hickory, larch, and red oak. I would stop by the chopped silage exhibit, where the hay is displayed in one-gallon glass jars so it can be judged for quality.

As twilight seeped over the fairgrounds, the lights of the midway grew brighter, and the incessant repetition of the barkers took over. Loud rock 'n' roll blared from the speakers as the mechanical rides whipped back and forth. When you were just two, Charlie, you played conductor on a small green train, a kindergarten ride that filled you with awe and pride. You grinned uncertainly as you passed your parents, who waved and took a half roll of snapshots, catching your small, beaming face as you rode by. Your older sisters begged to go one more time on the ride that snapped their thin bodies around, their faces contorted with centrifugal force and breathless fright, transported to another world. Their dreams were of lights and noise and blinding speed, of exhilaration at the end of a painted metal arm that slings them back and forth, up and down. My dreams are quieter these days, of the clicking of a horse-drawn mower, the clacking back and forth of the scythe bar, the hollow echoes of a workhorse's huge shod feet on the thick wooden floorboards of the stable.

As the country fair changes every year, I wonder what will become of the silence, the stillness of country life. I will miss those gallon jars of silage, small exhibits of the farming life to be put on a shelf forever, perhaps in a farm museum with the rope stretchers and milk testers. But for our family in a small valley in the Green Mountains of Vermont, the past is still the present. I still walk the barns of my childhood with you, my children, exploring the old cave at the mouth of the river, listening to the piercing, thin wailing of the coyotes as they come down out of the hollow toward the chicken coop just across the road. It is a haunting cry, bearing as much resemblance to the bark of a dog as the real west does to the rodeo at the fair. For now, the wild things still come out in the dark of night, two bears hoot at each other across the ridges behind our house, the red-tailed hawks circling in the late August afternoon sky, their keening a constant companion and reminder that there are things we still do not understand.

As I walked with you, Whitney, toward home one evening, through a field littered with fallen birch and poplar, you looked up at the circling hawk and sensed the connection, saying, "I wish it would drop us a feather." Although still a child, you wanted to reach out and touch the wildness, to carry the feather with you through life so when the hawk is gone and the silage jars are on museum shelves and the wilderness has retreated to just a memory, you can remember those days at the close of the twentieth century when you walked with your dad through the darkening hollow, when you looked up and saw a ghost in the sky and wanted to reach out and touch it.

When my turn comes, and I too am a ghost in the twilight, I hope to leave each of you a feather, memories of sudden storms and tall corn and quiet moments, walking hand in hand back home after a long summer day. It is my solemn responsibility to do this for each of you, for those who will live in a world after the last old-time Vermont farmer is dead and gone, committed back to the soil that will no longer raise crops or graze cows. I think that it is the earth itself you will miss most, the gravely scrabble or the rich loam of the river valleys. I often dream that those old farmers will lie there through the long winters and dry summers, whispering to you from their stony graves, their wordless song carried by the murmur of a brook or the rustle of leaves before a storm, calling us until we awake from our discontent, and the pastures once again feel the roots of young buckwheat, pushing down into the earth seeking moisture and inspiration.

PART SEVEN

Amazing Grace

forty-five

A fisher of children

"WITH CHILDREN, AS WITH FISH,
THE APPROACH IS EVERYTHING..."

---

n a cloudy August afternoon, the cry went up for a
fishing party. We dug for worms, rustled through the
barn for a net, checked the hooks and leaders, grabbed a few
poles, and we were soon off in the pickup, headed down to the
trout stream through a narrow back road that is closed in
winter. Each of you wore big rubber boots with red soles and
carried high expectations about who would catch the first fish.
The bed of the old truck jostled and shook independently from
the cab as we drove slowly over the narrow dirt track, up over
the mountain and then down again through a dark hollow.

Clouds sailed low over the mountaintops and a small field behind a white farmhouse disappeared into the mist. We rattled by the meadow where the last tribe of local Indians under Chief Chunks once made camp, a stand of curved white birch and poplar edging out into the grass. We drove deeper into the woods until we suddenly emerged onto the main road and turned left toward our fishing hole.

After the thrill of the first casts, we settled into a routine. Whitney, you took the project most seriously, checking your lure carefully—a Mepps or perhaps a Marble Spinner or a Sonic Rooster Tail. Caroline, you soon lost interest and, removing your boots, waded into the shallow current, looking for rocks and small fish. I crouched down next to you, Charlie, and helped you cast into the pool, amid cries of "Let me do it." Soon I was just a spectator, watching my three oldest children off on their own, enjoying the river each in their own way. Here I sat, a fisher of children, casting about with a great box of lures, applying all of the tricks I had learned in my lifetime to snare each of you with love, but also to prepare you for the rigors of adulthood. As you grow older, you will become harder to catch, like wild trout easily spooked by the slap of line on water or who have fickle tastes, the fly not perfectly matching the evening hatch. You will grow more patient with time, considering the bait before lunging. And once caught, you will put up a good fight, often running out the line or snagging it on a rock, the hook spit out and useless.

I must learn to be more clever as the years pass. I sit by the side of this famous trout stream and watch patiently, looking for a single rise in the still pool and choosing my fly carefully. With children, as with fish, the approach is everything. One poor cast and the fishing is over for the day, the waders stripped off and thrown back in the pickup for the ride home.

Whitney, you are an old trout who is always on guard, questioning hidden motives before I know I have them. You will only be caught willingly, taking the offered fly with full knowledge of the consequences.

Caroline, you are carefree but wily, keenly adept at manipulating others with breezy charm and false enthusiasm. You will take the fly that is offered out of sheer lust for life, enjoying the action; the great leaps from the water and the final landing, my hands holding you gently. You are no loner, no solitary brook trout content in your pool. When I reel you in,

I often realize that *you* have landed *me*. You are the fisherman in this family, the consummate player, the one who is most attuned to the whims and needs of others.

And then there is Charlie, who, still young, has enthusiasm and energy for all things. Every offering is worth a nibble and often a lunging strike. And once hooked, you are capable of a great fight, banging your head against the river bottom to dislodge an unwanted barb or running underneath the boat to tangle the line. You are a fisherman's dream, a hot streak of quicksilver, giving the fight of your life on every cast.

I think of other fishermen I have met over the years, their voices carrying clearly from a far shore or perhaps whispering encouragement at my side in the kitchen. They are unexpected visitors who pushed me into deeper currents before I knew I was ready, who used all the guile of an old angler to make me put up a good fight. And as I sit on the rocky shore, I watch each of my children and hope that they, too, will hear a voice, one that speaks to them about deeper currents. It will not be my voice. It will be an old hand who can cast a thousand yards, the fly kissing the surface of the water lightly, waiting patiently for those who are willing to rise to the occasion.

forty-six.

Be prepared

"WE ARE ALL PREPARING FOR WHAT LIES AHEAD,
FOR THE PROMISE OF ANOTHER WORLD..."

———————

On the shelf just above the board games and the cheap paperback novels, the sort of books that are well suited to a lazy summer afternoon, lies the tenth edition of *The Boy Scout Handbook*. I can see the red lettering down the spine from my chair, clear against a background of wood and pine needles. I pick it up and gaze for a minute at the icons placed carefully on the front and back covers—the baseball and bat, the Scout medals, the motto "Be Prepared," a compass, and photographs of scouts packing knapsacks, rappelling down a mountain, and rafting down a boiling river.

I flip through the pages and find instructions for lashing and splicing, for knots from hitches to bowlines, and for making a monkey bridge, a raft, or a desert water bag. The color illustrations demonstrate the difference between a red-tailed hawk and a Cooper's hawk, between a hog-nosed snake and a milk snake, between a white-tailed and black-tailed deer, and between the leaves of American elm, slippery elm, pawpaw, shingle oak, and persimmon, all of which look almost identical to me. The constellations are laid out for both the summer and winter sky, depending on whether one is looking north or south. Of course, there is much discussion of setting a course, using a map, and finding your way.

It is that last point—finding your way—which seems to be the subtext for the book, the more physical aspects of scouting being merely shadow play, good practice for the real challenges of life. Toward the back of the book, one gets into the meat of it, the discussion of taking initiative, the importance of learning, self-reliance, and good judgment, and the value of community and democracy. But it was the Scout law that really caught my attention. Here is the short version, which I hope you will take time to read:

A Scout is TRUSTWORTHY, telling the truth and keeping his promises. A Scout is LOYAL and true to his family and friends. A Scout is HELPFUL to other people and does not expect payment for assistance given. A Scout is FRIENDLY and accepts other people, and himself, for what they are. A Scout is COURTEOUS, or, put in simpler terms, a Scout is a gentleman. A Scout is KIND, understanding that one must truly listen to other people in order to be of help. A Scout is OBEDIENT and does not break the law of either the community or the land. A Scout is CHEERFUL and looks on the bright side of life. A Scout is THRIFTY and knows that he can live well with no more than the clothes he is wearing and the gear in his pack. A Scout is BRAVE, not only when faced with physical harm, but when speaking the truth or admitting a mistake. A Scout is CLEAN not only in body, but also in mind. A Scout is REVERENT, the wonders of the world constantly reminding him of the power and mystery of God.

Perhaps this abridged list of scouting values seems a bit old-fashioned or self-evident, but these twelve virtues have great resonance for a father at the end of the twentieth century.

This simple list is a good job description for your mother and I as we try to teach you about bravery and thrift, about being cheerful and never becoming discouraged, about how to be loyal and helpful. I would guess that a good teacher would dress up these lessons in more modern garb, making them entertaining. Yet any embellishment seems to me to be foolhardy. The great strength of simple truths is their simplicity, their bold-faced endurance that has weathered the storms of convenience and fashion. They are just as true today as they were a thousand years ago.

The Bible and *The Boy Scout Handbook* have much in common—both are guides to being prepared. Neither beguile through artifice but depend on the fact that eternal truths are self-evident and inherently powerful. As parents, we must prepare you for life. As children, you must also prepare for what lies ahead. Life can be lived more fully if one learns to distinguish between a simple mallard and a wood duck and between the fruits of the white oak, live oak, and black oak trees. One can also live a fuller life by being brave and honest, kind and cheerful, thrifty and helpful. Yet our lifetime of preparation has another purpose as well. We are all preparing for what lies ahead, for the promise of another world, which is described so eloquently in 1 Corinthians 2:9:

> NO EYE HAS SEEN,
>
> NO EAR HAS HEARD,
>
> NO MIND HAS CONCEIVED,
>
> WHAT GOD HAS PREPARED
>
> FOR THOSE WHO LOVE HIM.

Your mother and I can also promise you that in this world, there is much you have not yet seen, nor heard, nor conceived, and to discover the full promise of life all you have to do is be prepared.

forty-seven.

Sacred places

"ONCE FOUND, THE SACRED
IS EASY TO REDISCOVER…"

Before any of you were born, your mom and I always
tried to seek out unusual destinations, a Mayan ruin in
Guatemala or a fishing village in a backwater of the
Caribbean. However, now that we have four children, we have
set our sights on more family-friendly destinations—such as
the one we all traveled to recently, a resort in the British West
Indies replete with poolside cabanas, acres of fresh towels, and
possibly the most insipid food imaginable, beautiful but
without flavor or personality. Striking out on our own, we
dined exclusively at local eateries, almost always named after

their owners who took our orders, served our drinks, and then cooked our food. We cleaned our plates of parrot fish stewed in a sweet curry sauce, freshly grilled mahimahi, mounds of rice and peas, roasted plantains, toasted coconut slices as appetizers, rum punch made with fresh-squeezed lime juice, soursop ice cream, and a sandwich of flying fish served on thick slabs of homemade bread with fresh whisked mayonnaise and a large bowl of icy chocolate ice cream for dessert.

Although these eateries were visually unappealing— cinder block construction painted white, sagging rows of brightly colored Christmas tree lights lining the front walkway, Formica tabletops, the blare of CNN on the television, and faded color photos of tropical fruits on the walls—their spirit was filled with good home cooking, the soft gurgle of Carib beer being poured into glasses, the clatter of pans in the kitchen, and the cheerful presence of the proprietors. It occurred to me that some places are inhabited by the souls of their owners while others are empty shells, constructed only of sheetrock and two-by-fours.

On our last full day, we struck out to find a local church service and found ourselves in a district called Fig Tree, high up on the side of the dormant volcano, in a small Anglican church called St. George's. It was Palm Sunday, the fronds noisily whipped about by the white and blue electric fans set high on the columns. The church had no windows per se, just arched openings facing out onto an unkept graveyard, overgrown slabs of stone set flat on the ground. A few long, fluorescent lights lit the nave and the glassed-in organ pipes and a heavy, ripe scent of incense settled on us all, mixing with the humid, tropical air. The minister served three churches on the island and was blessed with a sonorous, booming voice that carried a tune and the sermon far out through the windows, languidly floating down onto the small, whitewashed houses fringing the ocean below.

After a few minutes, we all set out with the rest of the congregation, singing hymns in a procession along a mountain road with the altar boys in front and the minister in back, the notes from the organ fading as we descended. Here was a place truly lived in, I thought as I marched along with strangers, holding you, Charlie, in my arms, lungs filled with unfamiliar hymns, traffic stopped. A sacred place truly inhabited by the souls of its inhabitants.

When we arrived back in Vermont, it was mud season, in between the crisp, biting days of winter and the budding pale greens of springtime. Left behind were the rustling palms, the intense azure water, the moist, ripe flavor of the tropics. I set out on a short walk through a recently cleared field, water bubbling through the drainage ditches, weaving in and out of crisscrossed piles of newly cut locust, black birch, ash, and pine. The breeze was alternately warm, with a hint of wood smoke and boiling sap, Vermont's special incense, and then brisk, as if I had just stepped into a dark, frozen hollow.

And then bits of Anglican hymns came to me, the faded notes from the old organ still hanging in the air, and I was walking once again in a sacred place, with time suspended. Once found, the sacred is easy to rediscover, the cadence of birdsong as powerful as the rhythm of voices raised in chorus. Take the time to seek it out, on a walk in the country or in a sea of unfamiliar faces, the sacred appearing before you like a welcome friend.

forty-eight.

Too blessed to complain

"THE HAND OF GOD IS EASY TO FIND
IN OUR SMALL VALLEY..."

I remember the time our family attended a service at the Ebeneezer Baptist Church in the South End of Boston. Charlie, you were just a baby then, but Caroline and Whitney, you were dressed to the nines, knowing that this congregation takes Sunday services seriously. When we first stepped out of the mid-November wind into the warm, gothic sanctuary, it was like stepping off a plane onto a distant shore. It was all quite foreign—the male ushers dressed in black suits, white gloves, and bow ties; the women in starched white dresses; the ladies in hats, some squat and black, others wild, soaring with architectural abandon—but it was welcoming and stirring. And when the fired-up choirs got hold of "Have a Little Talk with Jesus," pumping it full of faith and harmony, each of you caught a bit of the spirit, never having experienced the full force of a Baptist choir.

In his sermon, the Reverend Kirk Jones spoke about a stranger he had met the other day in front of the church. He had asked her how she was, and she replied, "I'm too blessed to complain." As I thought about her words, it seemed to me that this was pretty good advice for living. Each of you is blessed with ample helpings of beauty and brains, with side orders of good humor and common sense. You are blessed with the love of two parents, the pale mountain sun lightly falling across your bed on summer mornings, and homemade biscuits for breakfast with thick peach jam. You come from a town with good New England families, such as Wilcox and Bentley, Skidmore and Croft. If you but stop for a moment, you can find whatever you are seeking in the gnarled trunk of an old crab apple tree or the sight of a rooster pacing down the dirt road by our house. The hand of God is easy to find in our small valley, barely concealed in the cold green water of our pond or the surprising scent of spearmint when sawing through the trunk of black birch.

As the service continued, I held our sleeping ten-month-old son in my arms and watched the lazy sunlight come and go through the soft green and yellow stained-glass windows, heard the strong, clear voices of witnesses testifying to their faith, noticed an impeccably dressed man with salt-and-pepper hair weeping softly in the pew ahead of me, and looked on as the red and yellow robed choir waved white paper fans donated by the nearby Davis Funeral Home. And then Caroline, you tugged on my sleeve and said, "Daddy, I think we're supposed to hold hands now." You were right—the congregation was holding hands, praying for the health of a sick member. As I gripped your perfect, small fingers, I suddenly realized that I was showered with the blessings of family, renewed by a five-year-old's soft touch. As we sang "We Gather Together," our souls were refreshed, the whole congregation coming together as one extended family. Truly, we are too blessed to complain.

forty-nine.

Peace be with you

"THIS SUNDAY RITUAL
WILL BE THERE WHEN YOU NEED IT,
FILLING YOUR HEART WITH FAITH WHEN IT IS EMPTY..."

The first Methodist church in our town stood across the street, moved from Ash Grove, New York, back in 1782. The current structure was erected in the 1870s, a modest church that holds no more than 150, although any sort of crowd is unusual these days. It was built on the edge of a cornfield, just off the main road into Beartown and not far from the river that contains the old Baptist hole. The congregation usually runs no more than twenty-five on a given Sunday, our family sometimes comprising a good percentage of those present. The walls are pressed tin painted white, the windows are high and narrow with the original, imperfect lights, the Green Mountains filtered in small bubbles of distortion, a child's attention held by the play of light and wavy glass. The artwork, Christ Blessing Little Children and Suffer Little Children to Come Unto Me, are modest, inexpensive prints of the biblical accounts. A few plaques also adorn the walls, the most practical reading, "Oil Burner Installed in May of 1972, John W. Lunquist."

Out in the small foyer, there is a smattering of mementos from the church's history: a Perkins Hollow Report Card from 1916 and photographs of Old Home Day, 1964, depicting hearty, broad-faced women with easy smiles and large flower-print dresses serving up dinner on long oilcloth-draped tables. I am drawn to those photos time after time, thirsty for the simplicity of those lives, faces open and expressive, sculpted by years of experience, like a large granite outcropping, weathered to a smooth, pleasing finish.

Each of you has been introduced to the congregation in turn, at first suckling at your mother's breast, oblivious to the world. And as you grow older, you fidget in your seat, trying to make out the words in the hymnal. When you turn three, you are excused with the other children after the first hymn for Sunday school, where you color scenes from the Bible—Jesus calling to the fisherman on the Sea of Galilee or overturning the tables of the money changers. And the day comes when you are presented with your own Bible, resplendent in its bright cardinal-red jacket, inscribed with your name, a gift from the minister and the congregation. For the most part, churchgoing is nothing more than ritual for you. Like some of the old-timers, you may come for the doughnut and biscuit during coffee hour or perhaps just for the bright crayons in the box in the back room. And some days you come just because you have to, your parents brushing your hair and shining your shoes as you wriggle and squirm, an unwilling traveler.

But soon enough, the Prayer for Thanksgiving and the Lord's Prayer and the ebb and flow of the morning service will become second nature. You will remember Charlie Bentley sitting in the back row, wearing his good suit and looking cheerful enough for a man more used to the metal seat on top of his Farmall. You will learn to shake hands with your fellow churchgoers and say, "Peace be with you," looking them straight in the eye and smiling. The view from the window by our pew will float through your dreams, the small wood cabin sitting just above the field planted alternately with corn or hay or alfalfa. You will see the Green Mountains in the distance, the clouds skimming over them on a Sunday morning, the sun suddenly lighting up this humble sanctuary, the Holy Spirit traveling at the speed of light to bring the good word.

The quiet and peace of this simple Sunday ritual will be there when you need it, filling your heart with faith when it is empty, clearing it of anxiety when it is crowded with angry thoughts. You will carry with you throughout life the sound of the furnace turning on and off in December, the chatter of neighbors during coffee hour, and the freedom of running with your friends through the field out the back door, the timothy higher than your heads. And you will walk through life to the back-and-forth cadence of "In the Garden" and hum the tune to the old Indian melody that now carries the words to "Amazing Grace." The songs will float back to you at unexpected moments, loose from their moorings in the simple white church, out the door, and into the ether that connects us all. Voices lifted high travel across the alfalfa and the corn, seeking us out, once again making a connection that brings us back home. And someday you will feel the Lord take your hand as I have taken yours in mine, and walk with you, and talk with you, and tell you that you are His own.

fifty.

Stopping by the cemetery

"DEATH IS A REMINDER
THAT THERE IS SO LITTLE TIME TO WASTE..."

Last summer, Whitney, you and I visited the Moravian cemetery late one afternoon. The sign was white with black paint, nailed to a post just by the stone wall that fronts the road. The grounds were overgrown, the leaves from a young poplar tree shading the sign from the bright sun. Once inside the cemetery gates, we walked on a deep pile of groundcover. Most of it was moss: rust brown and soft; other areas were carpeted by a dry, gray cover that crunched as we stepped gingerly between the gravestones. There were starbursts of yellow, small spikey flowers that grew up through the moss.

The land falls off in back, past the stone wall, to a lower field. A groundhog saw us and took off down the embankment, making good speed for a such a long, brown roll of fat.

The oldest gravestone we found belongs to Abraham Bininger, who was a missionary of the Brethrens Church, also known as the Moravians. He served in the West Indies and then lived among the American Indians. Born in 1720, Mr. Bininger "fell asleep in Jesus" at ninety-one years of age in 1811. But the saddest stones were those of young children. Mary Jane Blackwell passed in June of 1844 at just five years and eight months. Together we read this inscription:

This lovely plant so young and fair

Called home by early doom

Just come to show how sweet a flower

In paradise would bloom

Still, gravestones in Vermont often have a lighter side as well. My favorite stone, one that is up by the Methodist church, is for Fred Woodock Jr., who had an artist cut in drawings of those things he admired most in life—his dog, his cowboy hat, a harmonica, a plate of doughnuts, and a can of

Black Label beer. Others have carvings of a vintage Corvette or stern warnings to those who have survived them, reminding them of their impending doom, ending with dramatic admonitions such as "Be Prepared to Die!"

As I stopped to decipher a worn stone, I looked over and saw you picking wildflowers. You were taken with the grave of Mary Jane and laid the small bunch of Indian paintbrushes at the foot of her stone. You stood quietly and I guessed that children understand a great deal more about death than they let on. For many adults, death is a constant companion, proof that life is indeed without meaning. This is a narrow view of the universe, one based on the current theory that the universe is nothing more than chance, unknowable interactions between the stuff of life. But for others, death is the deep current that puts the fairy glow in the summer sunrise, a rare shining that lights the meadow by our house, the sun transforming the morning dew on stalks of timothy into a feathery web. Death is a reminder that there is so little time to waste. But it also gives us confidence in knowing that to spend an afternoon in a forgotten cemetery with a child is not time wasted.

I looked up and had a brief glimpse of quiet dignity as you stood solemnly by the grave of Mary Jane. Death had framed our afternoon together, but in expected ways. Perhaps it was the breath of wind, soft and hushed, or the late-afternoon sun providing drama to our small stage, but life was lived more keenly that day, amid the tombstones and ancient verse.

fifty-one

The Book of Wonders

"WONDER IS A PRECIOUS COMMODITY,
THE FRANKINCENSE OF OUR TIME..."

One of my favorite books as a child was *The Book of Wonders*, an encyclopedia of marvelous discoveries, from the monuments of the pharaohs to the mysteries of the duckbill platypus and the longnose bat. Centuries ago, many families displayed a wonder cabinet in their homes, filled with found treasures, from ancient coins, rare seashells, and butterflies to the simple four-leafed clover. In those days, the world was full of mysteries, places undiscovered, rumors of giant tusked mammals and rarely glimpsed tribes, sea monsters and the ends of the earth where the ocean might cascade into the void. The woods held secrets to be unlocked through careful study and observation, every leaf and insect having not been catalogued and yet put on display at the Smithsonian. Albert Einstein knew well that both science and life itself was only worth living in a rare envelope of mystery, for without it the imagination and life itself withers and dies.

For your mother and I, this farmhouse is full of wonder, each day replete with surprise and enlightenment. We wonder most about what immortal ether each of you came from, how the spark of life came to grace your small beings, mere mortal seed being lowly stuff compared to a holier spirit that lights your eyes and guides your way. Parents are no captains of their ship, merely the vessel itself, sturdy, predictable, and seaworthy but steered by other hands. It is a blessing to have the four of you as passengers on this journey, the two of us grateful and in awe at each passing mile.

We wonder at the mirror you hold up to us, reflecting bits of ourselves, a jigsaw puzzle of voice and eyes and attitude that have been randomly scattered among our offspring and then remolded into whole beings with secondhand parts cobbled together from the family tree. A glance here, an expression there combine to remind us that we have ties both to the past and future. No one person is able to live alone, unconnected to other generations. You are living proof that the thread of life is strong, binding us in a family web that eventually connects us all.

We marvel at the wonder you find in the coyotes who flow down from the ridges after midnight, their plaintive yapping filling your dreams, their dark shadows spilling over until daylight. You explore our brook and find the Amazon. A barn becomes a living museum built from the refuse of old farmers: mummified swallows, a horse-powered oat thresher, a pocketful of square-headed nails, and enough baling twine to stretch fifty times between bedposts, transforming a bed into a fortress. A bright orange salamander is an ambassador from another world, a reptilian kingdom that lies just below the surface of the forest. A bedtime story becomes a saga, one that makes no distinction between fact and fiction, the characters becoming part of the family legend, as real as the mailman or your Uncle Bud.

You live in an age of wonder, a world where the breath of the unseen is felt upon your neck, where the morning is fresh and full of possibilities, where, at any moment, something unspeakable might come crashing out of the woods. Each of you knows well that the universe is expanding toward infinity, that revelations may appear at sunset, the face of God suddenly forming in the whorls and wisps of glowing cumulus. The world has yet to be broken into its components, inspected, analyzed and then put away for reference. Each small component is still linked in some cosmic chain, the worm on the hook to the great black bears of your dreams, the orange and crimson of a sugar maple leaf to the east wind that brings a change of weather.

And as you mature, the wonder slips away slowly, poured, I hope, from your reservoir into ours, so not even one drop is spilled along the way. Wonder is a precious commodity, the frankincense of our time, and each generation is merely a trustee, a conservator of this rare stuff, the manna without which no life is worth living. And when you are older, a bit weary from the constant drumming of reality, your mother and I will open the sealed jar and pour forth this rich oil. We'll bathe your soul, rubbing the rich unguent into your temples and eyelids so that you may regain the eyes of a child and see the shadows in the mist,

sense the great rivers of wind that flow above the continents,

and find the face of God wherever you may look for it.

fifty-two.

May the good
Lord keep you

"FILL YOUR DREAMS WITH SWEET TOMORROWS..."

———————

ay the good Lord bless and keep you. He is also your father, one who will always be with you, whether near or far away. Whatever you seek in life, may you find that long-awaited golden day today. Each and every day in these Green Mountains brings the possibility of redemption, of stumbling upon satisfaction, like hooking onto a huge brown trout in a small brook. May your troubles all be small ones, but may you find strength and renewal in your troubles. If you do, you will find your fortune ten times ten.

Dear Charlie 239

Even in the darkest twilight, may you walk with sunlight shining and a bluebird in every tree, the tops of the red maples and shagbark hickory splashed with the glow of sunset. And don't forget to build and set out houses for the bluebirds while you are at it. We don't see so many around the farm anymore. And if you look after others, may there be a silver lining back of every cloud you see. Learn to appreciate all sorts of weather. Clouds bring rain for the corn and the timothy; snow means a good melt in the spring to build up the water table.

Fill your dreams with sweet tomorrows, but don't be an idle daydreamer. Remember that it is always today, never tomorrow, so never mind what might have been. You might have been a lot worse off, like the family down in New York State who lost a son under the tractor, or old man Vaughn who fell out of his hayloft and knocked himself silly. Remember to love your neighbor, or at least don't hunt on his property without permission. Be true to yourself and don't give a whit what others think of you, except the Lord. May He bless and keep you till we meet again.